The Workplace Where Everyone WINS

America's Huge Untapped Potential

JEFFERSON F. VANDER WOLK

ISBN 978-1-64114-939-6 (paperback)
ISBN 978-1-64114-940-2 (digital)

Copyright © 2017 by Jefferson F. Vander Wolk

All rights reserved. No part of this publication may be reproduced, distributed, or transmitted in any form or by any means, including photocopying, recording, or other electronic or mechanical methods without the prior written permission of the publisher. For permission requests, solicit the publisher via the address below.

Christian Faith Publishing, Inc.
832 Park Avenue
Meadville, PA 16335
www.christianfaithpublishing.com

Printed in the United States of America

CONTENTS

Preface 7
Introduction 17

Part I The Basics of Win-Win Management

Chapter 1   What's Wrong with Today's Workplace? 25
Chapter 2   Getting from Win-Lose to Win-Win 31
Chapter 3   A First Success: The Inn of the Governors Story 36
Chapter 4   Service Businesses: the Low-Hanging
            Fruit on the Road to the WWEW 44
Chapter 5   A Much-Delayed Second Success: the
            Waterway Cafe 49
Chapter 6   The Four Drivers of the WWEW 56
Chapter 7   The Benefits of the WWEW: Tangible
            and Intangible 62
Chapter 8   The Challenge of Implementing a WWEW 69

Part II Lessons from the Great Recession

Chapter 9   The Wisdom of Small Teams 77
Chapter 10 A Time for Painsharing 82

Endpiece: The Long-Term Potentials of the Workplace Where
     Everyone Wins 85
Epilogue 93
Acknowledgements 103
Appendix A 105
Bibliography 109
The Reason for this Book 111

To James F. Lincoln, W. Edwards Deming,
F. Kenneth Iverson, and John P. McConnell

PREFACE

Harvard Business School's Best-Kept Secret to Success

First published in 1947, the tale of one American company's success continues to resonate as Harvard Business School's most popular ever case study. Thousands of the world's most influential business owners, executives, journalists, and theorists have reflected on the story of this company's revolutionary business strategy for more than sixty years. The company profiled has remained true to its practices and unchallenged as the icon of its industry. Yet this company is not Coca-Cola, Procter & Gamble, or General Electric; it's not even a household name.

This singular story is that of the Ohio-based Lincoln Electric Company. Founded in 1895, it is today the world's largest manufacturer of arc welding equipment and related products—a multibillion dollar global company with manufacturing facilities in nineteen countries around the world. Yet, while aspiring or struggling—or even successful—business owners don't need to know the first thing about welding to appreciate Lincoln's philosophy and perhaps even duplicate its stunning performance, successful imitators have been virtually nonexistent.

What Did Lincoln Electric Do that was So Revolutionary?

What James Lincoln, the president of Lincoln Electric, had the fortitude to do in 1933, the pit of the Great Depression, was to make one change that transformed traditional cross-purposes and disaffection between labor and management into enthusiastic cooperation. That one change was to distribute the largest share of increases in profits beyond the prevailing norm to those doing the work. While this defied convention, it led in sequence to:

1. increases in worker productivity of up to 400 percent;
2. radical reductions in supervisory needs and employee turnover;
3. bonuses to all workers who, for more than seventy-five years, have averaged over 60 percent of base pay;
4. lower prices and better quality products for customers;
5. fast-growing market share for the company;
6. a commensurate increase in company earnings and the value of each investor's equity; and
7. a company culture so positive it once led to near-violent worker reaction to outsiders attempting—once, but never again—to unionize the company.

There is one point about this list of benefits that is perhaps too easy for business owners to overlook. It is the tremendous impact the trade-off of short-term profits can have on the long-term value of a company. This results from potentials to leverage both a much-enhanced income stream and the simultaneous creation of what is described in chapter 7 as a "magnificent business machine."

During the years leading up to World War II, while other manufacturers were struggling, Lincoln increased sales more than sixfold and assumed industry dominance. Household names like General Electric and Westinghouse were among those forced out of the electric welding business.

Among the few firms that have attempted profit sharing plans as radical as Lincoln's, the best known is the Nucor Corporation. In the late 1960s, Nucor, then known as Vulcraft, was a small, steel truss manufacturer—a division of the then-bankrupt Nuclear Corporation of America. By implementing a profit-sharing system much like Lincoln's, Vulcraft quickly achieved extraordinary levels of worker productivity.

Later, due to raw material issues, the company got into the steel business. Soon finding its high worker productivity allowed it to sell steel to others for less than their traditional sources, the company that became Nucor in 1972 began shifting its main focus to producing steel. Before long, many of our nation's largest steel producers—companies like Bethlehem Steel—were the ones on the road to bankruptcy. By 2004, Nucor had become America's largest steel producer. Along the way, it had made many investors very wealthy.

An amusing aside about Lincoln's approach came up during a discussion of its profit-sharing system at a Harvard Business School club in the Midwest. A union leader invited to join the discussion was quoted as saying, "Lincoln workers receive high pay and job security, and there is no need for a union there. But I'm not worried there will be a diminishing role for unions because most of you are too dumb to run your companies that way."

As recently discovered at two service companies, I had developed some time earlier and later turned into "experimental management laboratories," the issue this union leader raised is somewhat more complex than the word *dumb* suggests. The considerations underlying this issue and the reasons for this complexity will be fully addressed.

Yet, notwithstanding these considerations, this major question has remained: *Why have other manufacturers not lined up in droves to imitate Lincoln's approach, which has maintained its extraordinary success since the 1930s?*

Considering Lincoln's remarkable history and its continuing status as Harvard Business School's most popular case study, one would think that countless other manufacturers would have adopted its principles as their own. But not that many have even tried. Why?

Until now, other manufacturers familiar with Lincoln's success seem to have adopted a general (and now-proven premature) assumption that Lincoln's success was, as one put it, an "interesting anomaly." After all, Lincoln, like Nucor, instituted its highly cooperative management style during tough times when employee jobs were at risk. That had to moderate labor's understandable distrust when management "comes bearing gifts," trying to sell enthusiastic labor-management cooperation after years of cross-purposes and disaffection. Only now clear is that what Lincoln actually did was to tap a higher form of capitalism.

This point suggests why Harvard's multiple case studies of Lincoln have prompted such interest. Many of the thousands of people exposed to these studies have undoubtedly sensed that Lincoln's system had implications that extended far beyond this little known Ohio-based manufacturer of arc welding equipment.

Ironically, the system Lincoln developed was nearly accidental. According to a history of Lincoln Electric published by the company, it appears to have evolved from the sympathetic response of James Lincoln, the son of a minister, to a question posed to him by an employee-member of his company's advisory board. That question: "Mr. Lincoln, if we worked harder, could you pay us more money?"

Lost in the history of what followed has been the point that Lincoln never designed its system to be used by other manufacturers nor, for that matter, by service organizations, either. In fact, a second premature assumption, seemingly resulting from piecework being a component of Lincoln's bonus system, was that the system would never work in a service business. Also lost over the decades has been a key question that has gone unanswered by even the Harvard guys: *Why has virtually no other company (except Nucor and Worthington Industries, perhaps) ever duplicated the success enjoyed by Lincoln?*

The quick easy answer is that the response-times or feedback loops in manufacturing are so slow, they serve to reinforce the normal distrust of workers. This discourages manufacturers from offering financial benefits to their employees, like those offered by Lincoln—absent the kind of job loss threats faced by employees at Lincoln and Nucor. These slow feedback loops and the resulting delay in major bonus payouts (once a year at Lincoln) make the adoption of any approach as radical as Lincoln's a tall order. Understandably, successful manufacturers, instead of seeing Lincoln's success as the function of a higher form of capitalism, chose to view it as an anomaly. This paved the way for them to conclude about their traditional win-lose management model: "If it ain't broke, don't fix it."

The better—not "dumb"—answer to why manufacturers, generally, never tried to duplicate Lincoln's success came to light recently in my two management laboratories. This answer turned out to have two dimensions: The first arose from the discovery that with one simple change, Lincoln's philosophy cannot only work but work wonders in service businesses. The second arose from the discovery that because service businesses usually enjoy very fast feedback loops, Lincoln's philosophy is far easier to install in most service businesses than in manufacturing.

This latter observation produces the clear implication that the service sector is where the low-hanging fruit is found, which needs to be picked first if a system as radical as Lincoln's is to gain traction in the more-challenging realm of manufacturing.

The way I came to these conclusions began with the often-overlooked recognition that most systems designed by humans—of which Lincoln's is clearly one—are open to evolution. This, coupled with strong hints that Lincoln had in fact unveiled a higher form of capitalism, suggested that its approach was not the end-all model seemingly assumed but only a first-generation version of better things likely to come. This further implied that Lincoln's system was no more a predictor of what is possible than the airplane flown by the Wright brothers at Kitty Hawk was a predictor of today's jet airliners and space vehicles.

Our development of a second-generation model has shown that, besides its ease of installation in service firms, these firms can quickly achieve, relative to base pay, the level of bonus awards (we call them gain-shares) that Lincoln achieved in manufacturing. In addition, these bonus awards can be made to employees—in our case monthly—before they have much time to even think about the motives of management.

This second-generation model should be easier for manufacturers to adopt than was the first-generation model. Even if not, however, two positive outcomes seem certain: First, awareness of the benefits of this new model is bound to spread as its use goes forward in the service sector. Second, awareness of these benefits will not go unnoticed by the employees of manufacturers, who in time will start pressuring their employers to adopt the same model. Over time, as this employee pressure builds, the position of manufacturers that "if it ain't broke, don't fix it" is bound to give way to "we'd better join the parade before our competitors do or risk following into bankruptcy those companies sent there by Lincoln and Nucor."

As was the case with Lincoln and its first-generation model, this second-generation model came about with one simple change. This was to replace piecework (the number of actions performed by a worker in a given amount of time) with team performance as not just a factor but the major factor in bonus awards.

This modification of Lincoln's approach cannot only move any workplace culture from win-lose to win-win but can open it to synergies of teamwork that, with few exceptions, have been inaccessible under the traditional win-lose model of management. Because of the cross-purposes and related disaffection inherent in the win-lose model, high-performance teams have been rare. They have usually appeared only by chance in small groups of uniquely compatible individuals.

Even at that, such successes have tended to be ad hoc teams that have disbanded as soon as a single team objective was achieved. Such random successes seem the exceptions that prove the rule in companies under traditional win-lose management. The limiting attitude was expressed—and hopefully overstated—by the title of a 1970s book by Robert Townsend, the president of Avis. Its title, *Up the Organization*.

By contrast, in the second-generation model of what Lincoln started, supervisors become coaches, and the folks doing the work become operating partners in the business, sharing a common purpose with the owners. This culture of sharing creates an ideal infrastructure for permanent teams, with each team enjoying a potential to create, over time, increasingly high performance.

Besides their tangible benefits, high-performance teams have proven to be notable sources of mutual empathy and interpersonal commitment among teammates. With no cap implied on the growth of these intangible values, various interesting questions arise about the potential of a third- or fourth-generation upgrade of Lincoln's system to impact in a major way how human beings relate to one another.

Our two management laboratories are the one-hundred-room Inn of the Governors—with its popular, high-value Del Charro restaurant—in Santa Fe, New Mexico, and the recently expanded four-hundred-seat Waterway Cafe in Palm Beach Gardens, Florida. Based on published customer reviews, both are consistently rated by Trip Advisor at or near the top among like facilities in their respective cities. In stable times, both of these laboratories have qualified as cash cows, with earnings well exceeding those of like properties. Contributing factors, beyond the obvious benefits of their second-generation operating systems, include very low staff turnover and general managers who are on board to stay. Which likely explains why the oversight needs of owners, absent a major calamity or large capital spending program, can be very limited. This means that owners, rather than spending typically large amounts of time with their representatives on operating issues, can utilize that time more productively on strategic growth considerations.

So how have things worked out at what have been the specific results at these two management laboratories?

To start, I would emphasize that everyone involved with these businesses is either an operating partner or an investment partner. Operating partners are all of those—including onsite managers—involved in the day-to-day operation of these businesses; investment partners are those who provide or have provided the capital needed to create or expand them.

We instituted this structure at both properties in 2004. In just one year, the Waterway Cafe's gainsharing rate to every staff member reached $300 monthly—or $3,600 annually. At that point, we encountered some unique circumstances beyond our control: They started with a thirty-month state of Florida project to rebuild the bridge adjoining our property, reducing traffic lanes from six to two, often none; during this period came the unprecedented development of seventy new restaurants within two-plus miles west of us; and, finally, three hurricanes in quick succession. By the time these events passed, the Great Recession was upon us. Fortunately, our management system has succeeded in keeping our relative performance well above that of our competitors.

The Santa Fe hotel took a bit longer to build its early gainsharing rate because of the slower feedback loops inherent in hotels. However, by the time the recession arrived in 2008, this property was providing a $670 monthly gainsharing—a rate of over $8,000 annually—to every staff member, including maids and dishwashers. Much of this gainsharing rate came from increasing the hotel's revenue per available room (average room rate multiplied by occupancy) from just over 100 percent of the downtown Santa Fe average to 137 percent of that average.

During these four years, the inflation-adjusted return to the owners rose from $1.8 to $2.3 million. While profits at the other downtown Santa Fe hotels, based on roughly 10 percent inflation, appear to have fallen by about 5 percent, our profits, including gainsharing payouts, rose from $1.8 million to just over $3.0 million.

The good news since 2008 is that both properties have maintained their dramatically low rates of staff turnover, and after some adjustments to reflect a new norm in business at both locations, our staffs have their gainsharing on an upward march once again.

So how do we view the longer-term potentials of what Lincoln started?

To begin, one needs to fully appreciate the chain of past failings that has blocked for seventy-five years the spread of the higher form of capitalism unveiled by Lincoln in 1933. The first—and root cause of this delay—has been the failure of American business to recognize that Lincoln's approach was open to evolution. This abetted the beliefs, first, that Lincoln's success was an anomaly and, second, that its approach would never work in service businesses. In turn, this latter belief blinded us to the fact that service is not only where this strategy is the easiest to install, but if it is to further spread, it needs to be implemented first

THE WORKPLACE WHERE EVERYONE WINS

Given these insights, what is now indicated? With cross-purposes between labor and management still the norm in virtually all businesses, the potentials are huge. Tapping them needs to get underway with the second-generation version of Lincoln's approach in service firms—to then be accompanied by a logical progression into manufacturing.

This path would also start to tap broader potentials to reverse the many negative trends that now afflict our nation. These include our debt and deficits, negative balance of trade, the decline of both our manufacturing base and the value of our currency, our regulatory overload, etc. Along with this would come countless intangible benefits.

Had such a revolution in management practice unfolded following the Great Depression and World War II, we would by now be living in a very different and far more positive world, economically, politically, and socially. While missing this opportunity is regrettable, the good news is that it is still knocking at our door, waiting to be exploited.

INTRODUCTION

Like most others with an entrepreneurial bent, I started out in business at age twenty-five wanting to make a lot of money. Unlike most others, perhaps, I felt that making money should be my primary goal only up to a point. I wanted many of the things money can buy like fine seasonal homes in warm, attractive places, nice automobiles, an offshore sailboat, a fast airplane, membership in clubs with like-minded friends and, not least, enough savings to secure this lifestyle. But beyond these things, my priorities shifted dramatically. I wanted lots of free time for other interests. I also wanted to remain active in business—but not in a way that making money would be the primary driver.

Given the benefit of a business school education, I had planned to go to Wall Street, but that plan was delayed and ultimately scrapped because of a Korean War tour of duty in the air force.

By a stroke of good fortune, I was sent, as a totally green jet instructor pilot, to Webb Air Force Base, next to the small, dusty city of Big Spring, Texas. When graduating from pilot training near Phoenix, Arizona, my fellow pilots had expressed great sympathy for my assignment to an area they considered the world's jumping-off place. But I was happily surprised when I arrived at my new destination to find that it was a short commute from the city of Midland, which, in 1955, was an oil boomtown of fifty thousand people. It was a place of unique business opportunities that had attracted a long parade of Ivy League fortune-seekers, including George H. W. Bush and his family.

With my duty as a flight instructor requiring only half-days—either mornings or afternoons—I was soon living in Midland, commuting to Big Spring and, in my free time, scouting for business opportunities in Midland. One obvious need was for more housing. Young families were virtually standing out in the rain in hopes of finding a home. So I enrolled in a course with International Correspondence Schools on how to build a house (earning the only A of my academic career). At the same time, I talked to an old buddy from New England, a talented sales type, into joining me in Midland. We were soon building houses and, within a year, starting to develop subdivisions. The air force had unknowingly provided a great opportunity.

When the housing boom started to cool four years later, my partner and I began building rental apartment and commercial projects in Midland and other cities. Also, with Midland's only downtown hotel dating to the 1920s, its largest savings and loan association approached us with an offer we couldn't refuse—a mortgage that would fully cover the cost of building a new hotel. We, of course, accepted and were soon developing, alongside Midland's many highrise office buildings, what would become a 120-room Sheraton Inn. We knew nothing about running a hotel, but the great popularity and profitability of the Inn's "pub"—a design fashioned after a classic Ivy League hangout—created the impression we knew what we were doing.

By age thirty-five, through both good luck and hard work, I was well on my way to achieving my financial goals. Further, my partner of ten years was into other things. So I decided to stop developing income properties in the Southwest and go into semiretirement on the East Coast. I had two goals in mind—one hopefully short-term, the other obviously long-term.

My Short-Term Goal

I wanted to learn how to successfully manage from the East Coast the properties we had developed in the Southwest with a minimum commitment of my personal time.

I was aware from the start that this arrangement would require the kind of employee trust and cooperation that eludes virtually all traditional relationships between labor and management. However, it seemed like the perfect opportunity to experiment with a management approach that had long fascinated me. This approach involved exactly this kind of trust and cooperation among everyone involved. At that time, I knew of only one company that had achieved this. It was the Lincoln Electric Company. I had in fact read about the company and visited with Mr. Lincoln on my way to cadet training in the air force.

I found Mr. Lincoln a very nice man who was generous with his time. I left feeling I would try to incorporate his philosophy into any business I might develop. The only truly stable businesses I later developed, however, were service businesses. And, unfortunately, the conventional wisdom was that Lincoln's approach, which included the use of piecework in awarding bonuses, would never work in a service business. So, for a long time, I put Lincoln's philosophy on the back burner.

My Longer-Term Goal

While I had found making money a lot of fun and was most appreciative of the opportunities that had come my way, making more money was no longer my primary concern. I would gladly accept whatever came my way, but I was not inclined to chase after more than I needed to fund and secure my first-stated goals. And beyond pursuing my short-term management objective, I wanted to take on something more challenging.

I had in fact chanced upon two related questions that most would regard as too esoteric to consider. But assuming I would have plenty of time, I was looking for a real challenge. These two questions fit that description. Their source was George Gurdjieff, an obscure Russian philosopher who created a major stir among intellectuals in Europe and America in the 1920s and '30s, with his two-part question: What is the purpose of life on earth and human life in particular? These seemed two issues not only worth pursuing but not likely to yield quick answers. To date, while this search remains far from its goals, the analysis it required of how controllable systems evolve is what finally forced me to conclude that Lincoln's approach was open to evolution.

Back to Shorter-Term Realities

Returning to my goal of finding how to operate apartments, hotels, and restaurants from distant locations with a minimum commitment of time, I was making less progress and taking more time than I had expected. Over twenty-five years, I developed several cost control systems that could be applied progressively, as needed or desired, to get a specific result. But the feeling persisted that what I was trying to achieve would be so much easier if I could get everyone rowing the boat in the same direction—right down to the maids and dishwashers.

Near the end of this twenty-five-year period, an event occurred that would start putting Lincoln's philosophy back on my front burner. In the early 1990s, I was invited by Bill Glavin, the president of Babson College, to join their board of trustees. Bill, a very dynamic former vice-chairman of Xerox, was a strong advocate of the management ideas of W. Edwards Deming, the "quality guru" generally seen as the person most responsible for Japan's economic miracle following World War II. Glavin had used Deming's ideas to help build Xerox and had started applying the same ideas at Babson. Before long, Babson was being ranked the top entrepreneurial school in America, a status it continues to enjoy.

At my first board of trustees meeting, several freshmen who had just attended a summer retreat that focused on Deming's ideas reported their reactions. While my knowledge of these ides was very limited, I was so impressed by the enthusiasm of these eighteen-year-olds, I returned home and immediately ordered and read several books about Deming. That was the start of my connecting certain dots that, in time, led me to two key conclusions: first, that if Lincoln's approach was modified by incorporating certain of Deming's ideas, it could likely be made to work in service businesses; second, that the service sector, because of its fast feedback loops, is where Lincoln's approach needs to be installed first if it is ever to acquire sufficient credibility to gain traction in manufacturing and ultimately proliferate throughout our economy.

These were auspicious conclusions. They not only led me to fully realizing my original short-term goal but to countless other benefits, tangible and intangible, both for myself and my employees. Hopefully, what follows will help bring similar benefits to growing numbers of other owners and their employees.

PART I
The Basics of Win-Win Management

CHAPTER 1

What's Wrong with Today's Workplace?

The key question isn't what fosters creativity? It is why in God's name isn't everyone creative? Where was this human potential lost? How was it crippled?"
—*Abraham Maslow (psychologist)*

When two countries wage war, it is not hard to see the resulting losses: the tremendous waste of resources that could have been put to positive use and the physical destruction and/or loss of life so often suffered on both sides. When there is no active warfare, however, and countries simply harbor negative biases and feelings toward each other, we can easily miss seeing the lost potentials.

Disaffection between countries is so common that we don't even try to assess the cost of such lost potentials or consider the possible benefits of cooperation. On those rare occasions where someone fashions a creative breakthrough between two nations that taps the potentials of cooperation, we tend to be surprised, even amazed. Such win-win thinking is a violation of the norm. But soon, our consciousness settles back into the noncreative realms of win-lose thinking.

Such disaffection between countries is not unlike the disaffection that has long existed in varying degrees in labor-management relations in our society. Again, this disaffection leads into win-lose biases that take a huge, obviously accepted, toll on both sides. The mind-set that settles in is the same one that said Lincoln Electric was an "interesting anomaly," a violation of the norm. Not only does this mind-set require a denial that there might be a better way to do things but a refusal to examine the circumstances. While fully defining such self-limiting mind-sets could take more than a single book, hopefully the following summary will stir interest in exploring alternative possibilities. What follows is just a sampling of the effects of win-lose thinking, so we'll start with a brief overview before proceeding to some of the specifics.

The Basic Problem: Productivity Far Below What It Might Be

When owners and managers operate with the win-lose mentality of traditional capitalism, they are engaged, whether they realize it or not, in a zero-sum game with their employees. Viewed objectively, this conventional relationship between labor and management is so flawed one would think the advantages of a win-win relationship would have long ago become apparent.

Over time, the traditional win-lose relationship—and related mind-sets of management and labor—have created two conflicting cultures in the workplace. On the one hand, the culture of management is focused on winning the game of higher earnings and taking all the chips. In addition, management often views labor as simply a replaceable commodity. Seldom has such management seen workers as potentially creative human beings capable of bringing forth continual improvement in their businesses if given significant incentives.

On the other hand, there is the worker culture. Workers in a win-lose system tend to feel a lack of recognition and respect from management and see themselves as mistreated or even cheated. As a result, they tend to become disaffected, apathetic, or even antagonistic.

These opposing cultures result in a huge loss of potential productivity in both manufacturing and service organizations.

For example, because of the win-win style of management practiced at Nucor, their employees became dramatically more productive than their counterparts at the big, highly respected and traditionally managed steel companies. Virtually all of Nucor's major competitors were eventually forced to close their doors.

Productivity in service businesses is less clear because good and bad service cannot be quantitatively measured. We can recognize great service and how rare it is. We can also recognize terrible service, which, unfortunately, is far too common—even in some of the more prestigious service businesses. On a scale of one to one hundred, not too many of today's service people appear to deserve a rating above fifty. All too many reflect the kind of indifference to customer needs and desires that would rank them at the lower levels of the scale.

This indifference, usually the result of disaffection and cross-purposes with management and its win-lose system, exists not just in service businesses but in virtually all businesses. Here are some of the typical outcomes:

• *The Fixed-Pie Syndrome.* One of the more common outcomes of win-lose management is known as the fixed-pie syndrome. It leads to a certain blindness on the part of both labor and management to ways of improving productivity and increasing profits. Instead of seeing potentials to "grow the pie," both sides, given limited incentives to cooperate, take the position that if the other side gets more, they get less. And as these fixed positions come into play, major potentials for continual improvement and higher earnings go out the window.

One case of this came to light several years ago when a manufacturing company offered a significant reward to any employee whose suggestion for improvement resulted in the company saving money. A suggestion from two long-standing employees who had worked together for many years on a key operation turned out to produce annual savings of over $500,000. When asked how long they had been aware of this savings potential, the answer was "about fifteen years."

Though obviously exceptional, this case illustrates how even the softest of biases, plus apathy about cooperation with management, can block the improvement of both productivity and creativity. The traditional mind-set that settles in goes a long way toward answering the questions at the beginning of the chapter posed by psychologist Abraham Maslow.

Thus, we should not be surprised by the lack of vision on both sides of the labor-management divide about many untapped potentials lost in traditional capitalism. Optimistically, one might hope that increasing recognition of these untapped potentials might lead over time not only to huge increases in worker productivity but to the reversal of the many negative trends afflicting our nation. Absent progress toward reversing these trends, America's future prospects look less than robust.

More Specifics

When labor and management are operating in the traditional win-lose mode, it is no exaggeration to say that the losses are legion. They include:

• *Lack of loyalty*. Instead of management and labor working as a team with a shared purpose, management's claim to essentially all of any expanding profits undercuts worker loyalty. An uncooperative attitude among workers is often encouraged by labor union work rules. This lack of loyalty nourishes a divisive mentality that often leads workers to become cynics, critics, bystanders, and even blamers. They do only what they are forced to do, and some tend to complain to fellow workers about virtually everything.

• *Lack of employee creativity*. The unspoken understanding in traditional capitalism is that the boss knows best. Workers are expected to leave their brains at the door and simply do as they are told. As a result, there is no worker commitment to continual improvement but only to performing the minimum required. Tremendous potentials go untapped.

• *Employee theft.* In restaurants, stories of workers walking out the back door with steaks in their pockets and bartenders giving free drinks to their buddies are endless. There was a famous World War II story about a Fisk Tire plant where night-shift workers were throwing newly finished tires out the window into the river below while their confederates downstream picked up the floating tires and sold them on the black market.

Innumerable other forms of theft are practiced continually in both manufacturing and service businesses.

• *Absenteeism.* In a win-lose climate, many people do not feel very obligated to show up at work. One result: they take as many sick days as possible.

• *Employee turnover.* If job security and pay are not protected by a labor union, employees, especially those with demanding supervisors, tend to become easily discouraged and often just pick up and leave.

• *Increased stress.* In any antagonistic win-lose climate, resentment and anger, along with the stress they create, are usually present. This atmosphere of negative emotions is bound to affect both labor and management, leading to loss of enthusiasm, lack of energy, inefficiency and, over time, burnout for many staff members.

• *Fear.* In traditional capitalism, many employees tend to perform as much out of fear as positive motivation. They fear being fired or demoted if they do not meet arbitrary standards. On the other hand, their own fellow employees, especially if union members, may threaten them if they appear to promote management's goals. While labor unions eliminate fear up to a certain point by protecting jobs, they can also create stress and conflict among employees. This is especially true when a union calls a strike or forces a lockout without the support of all its members.

• *Loss of customer loyalty.* Simple apathy among a labor force in a win-lose relationship with management consistently leads to failure to do the things that would increase quality and efficiency in the business. Instead, especially in service businesses, it often leads to behavior that displeases or annoys customers. Creating positive people connections is seldom seen as part of a service person's job. Service employees such as waiters and receptionists in a restaurant seldom recognize they are key "marketing people." Often, they can make or break a business.

The Bottom Line

By bridging the traditional divide between labor and management, Lincoln and Nucor eliminated or dramatically reduced these downsides of conventional capitalism. They did it in manufacturing businesses.

This book affirms that not only can the workplace culture they achieved be created in service businesses but that it can be created much faster and more easily in a service business than in manufacturing. This opens doors never before opened.

CHAPTER 2

Getting from Win-Lose to Win-Win

Lincoln, Nucor and Their Win-Win Cultures

The Industrial Revolution took root in the United States in the early 1800s. Over time, it led to everything, from bloody union busting to paternalistic company unions designed to fend off outside unionization. These company unions were ultimately outlawed by the National Labor Relations Act of 1935.

By 1933, the Lincoln Electric Company, founded in 1895, had no company union, but it did have an advisory board comprised of cooperative representatives from both labor and management The president of the company, James F. Lincoln, was the son of a minister and a staunch believer in the Golden Rule. Thus, he was sympathetic when, in the depths of the Great Depression, a frontline worker on the advisory board asked, "Mr. Lincoln, if we worked harder, could you pay us more money?" This simple question marked the beginning of an incentive plan unique in the history of industrial relations.

In the case of Nucor, its recorded life started as Vulcraft, a small division of a soon-distressed parent company, the Nuclear Corporation of America. The Vulcraft division manufactured steel trusses used in commercial buildings.

At a meeting of executives called in the late 1960s to address the parent company's bankruptcy prospects, Ken Iverson, president of Vulcraft, volunteered to try to save the parent company from its imminent fate. His offer was quickly accepted.

Iverson immediately sold off all of Nuclear Corporation but the Vulcraft division and implemented an incentive system much like Lincoln's. And, like Lincoln, it was soon enjoying remarkable worker productivity. In time to guarantee a reliable supply of quality steel, Nucor began producing its own steel. Soon finding it could sell steel to others for less than current market prices, it began expanding its steel-producing operations. Before long, it was on its way to becoming America's largest steel producer and repeating on a much grander scale the pattern that had unfolded at Lincoln. By 2003, the market value of Nucor common stock, which had by then made many investors wealthy, was about ten times that of Lincoln.

Factors to Consider

One should keep in mind, when thinking about the "workplace where everyone wins" (to which we have given the acronym, WWEW) is that it is still a work-in-progress, open to improvements yet to be identified.

This potential for improvement was made abundantly clear in our service businesses during the first two years of the recession that took hold in 2008. Whereas Lincoln Electric, which enjoyed unrestricted access to broader markets, was able to keep increasing sales in difficult times, our two service businesses, lacking this broader potential, suffered declining revenues.

Sales at both of our restaurants in the first twelve months of the recession were off by 10–15 percent. While this was somewhat less than declines suffered by competitors, our profits fell by close to one-half of the dollar amount of lost sales. Room profits at the Santa Fe hotel suffered an even greater decline as competitors lowered their room rates. In spite of having only 36,500 room nights to sell annually, we felt we had no choice but to match these rate reductions.

On the brighter side, while we reduced the hours of work for some hourly employees, we were seemingly the only Santa Fe hotel not to lay off any employees. One reason was that our abnormally high room occupancy never declined.

One positive outcome of the recession was recognizing that our system had a key potential for improvement that we had totally overlooked. It was to restructure our eighty-to-one-hundred-member teams at each location into far more effective five-to-twelve-member teams. Since, as WWEWs, we already had a partner-like relationship with our employees, these smaller teams created a unique potential to pursue high-performance teamwork. One of many good things such teamwork can create is the kind of "glue" with guests and customers that can often transcend price. This program is underway.

Resistance to Change

Another point to keep in mind when implementing a WWEW is the normal resistance to change that can be encountered in almost any business. Resistance increases whenever the introduction of a new system requires reversals of long-established thinking and practices. Such resistance was clearly a factor among manufacturing executives who, when hearing Lincoln's remarkable story, chose to regard its success as an historical accident.

Service businesses implementing a WWEW are, in theory, subject to the same resistance problem. It is largely mitigated, however, by faster feedback loops and greater staff adaptability in service firms than in manufacturing.

Staff adaptability in service businesses is higher because so many service employees tend to be young, highly mobile, and more open to new ideas. At the extreme of low staff adaptability are older manufacturing employees, often working under established union work rules that limit increases in productivity. That is why the prospects for use of the WWEW in manufacturing are largely limited at this time to companies with exceptional leadership.

One such company that, early on, adopted a win-win approach was Worthington Industries, a highly successful start-up steel parts manufacturer where there was no disaffection because, among other things, its owner, John McConnell, had a do-unto-others business philosophy.

Resistance to change, however, can be expected to remain strong among most well-established and successful manufacturers. Before this resistance will soften, the benefits of abandoning long-held mind-sets and embracing a win-win style of management will have to gain wider recognition among both labor and management.

Seeing the Benefits of Change

That employees can easily adapt to reversals in past practices is but one of several factors that make it easier for service businesses to successfully implement a WWEW.

Another factor is that service businesses can deliver to their employees the financial benefits of growing productivity far more quickly than typical manufacturers. In restaurants, for example, these benefits can be generated so quickly that employees will realize the positive potentials open to them virtually before they have time to think about resisting change.

Because restaurants are involved in both the service businesses described in this book, and because they are among the candidates best suited for implementing a WWEW, restaurants are given more attention than other service businesses in what follows. While hotels may take slightly longer than restaurants to generate the benefits of this higher system, they will be given due attention. One advantage hotels enjoy over restaurants is a much higher percentage of profit on each dollar of additional room revenue a WWEW can deliver.

Productivity in Service Businesses

Worth noting here is that productivity in service businesses involves, beyond superior performance in all operational aspects, the specific ability of employees to develop positive connections with both customers and fellow staff members. Fortunately, both of these productivity outcomes evolve naturally from implementing a WWEW and striving for ever-improving teamwork.

Theoretically, with only two successful examples to cite of the WWEW in service businesses, one might expect these examples to encounter some of the same attitude of "historical accidents" that greeted Lincoln's success. However, the templates of the WWEW are so simple and the benefits so self-evident, particularly in restaurants and hotels, that most owners should be able to implement a WWEW with relative ease. They should face little, if any, of the resistance to change manufacturers could presently expect to encounter.

These two service sector cases leave little doubt about the powerful advantages of restructuring the traditional distribution of expanding company profits along the lines of Lincoln's model. While Mr. Lincoln related his company's success largely to the Golden Rule, other company officers made clear that altruism was not the only reason for instituting the company's incentive system. Nucor's Ken Iverson, in his book, *Plain Talk*, framed his motivation quite simply, noting, "There comes a point where you need to get your hands out of the pockets of the people doing the work."

The Common Pattern

In simplest terms, Lincoln and Nucor, as well as our two service businesses, have transformed typical labor-management disaffection in the workplace into growing cooperation. With this cooperation, all four of these organizations did more than create customer delight and high monetary returns for both staff and owners. They created positive company cultures where everyone was not only winning but relating to each other in increasingly positive ways.

Over time, the installation of the WWEW in more and more service businesses can lead to wide worker recognition of the system's benefits. In turn, this can open the door to the evolution of this style of management not only in service businesses but in most businesses.

In what follows, I will explain in more detail how our two "management laboratories," the Inn of the Governors and the Waterway Cafe, became workplaces where everyone wins.

CHAPTER 3

A First Success: The Inn of the Governors Story

Soon after cutting our teeth on the hotel business in Midland, my partner and I were planning to build some rental apartments in New Mexico. So we went to Santa Fe to apply for a state contractor's license. While it was the dead of winter and the pit of the tourist off-season, we had trouble finding a hotel room in the downtown area. So while I dealt with the licensing needs (nothing compared to today's bureaucratic demands), my partner scoured the downtown area for possible hotel as well as apartment sites.

We had just entered into an eight-four-year ground lease on a prime apartment site in Albuquerque and had in mind doing the same in Santa Fe. Leasing the land was a great way to reduce required development funds above a typical mortgage—as long as the landowner agreed to a one-time subordination of his interest in the property to a first mortgage.

With some guidance from the Santa Fe building inspector, my partner found a top downtown site for a hotel. It was right at the end of the historic Santa Fe Trail.

In earlier times, it had been the site of Closson's Stable and, later, a Buick dealership owned by the same family. The dealership had relocated to the outskirts of town, and the Closson family wanted to sell or lease the acre-plus site. So we showed the family's lawyer a copy of our just-completed Albuquerque lease, which included the desired provision for one-time subordination to a first mortgage and proposed to enter into a similar lease on the vacant Buick site. Since the Albuquerque lease had been drawn up by a well-known and highly respected Albuquerque lawyer—also a major landowner there—the Santa Fe lawyer soon approved the lease. We were off to the races with our second hotel project.

The hotel's site was across a mostly dry creek bed ambitiously named the "Santa Fe River" from the state capitol complex. So Frank Welch, the talented architect we retained, adopted the same territorial building style as the capitol, and we named the project the Inn of the Governors. The name was a bit of a stretch, perhaps, since the property, which opened for business in 1965, might best be described as an upgraded Holiday Inn. Its eighty rooms were relatively small, with two-thirds of them on outside corridors exposed to the sometimes-harsh Santa Fe winters. The property's bar, the Forge, duplicated the Pub in our Midland property. And, as in Midland, the bar became so popular it paid the mortgage and then some for quite a few years. The restaurant, though attractive, produced food of mediocre quality. Like most small hotel restaurants, it was a mild drain on profits.

During these early years, Santa Fe was a small city of about fifty thousand residents. It was considered a regional tourist destination that, because of a limited water supply, was not expected to experience very much growth.

Finding the Right Manager

Like most hotels, the Inn suffered frequent manager turnover. In our first ten years, we went through five managers. By then, I realized that if we were going to make the property a significant and enduring success, we needed to find a committed long-term manager. So I began a serious search.

Having used a professional head-hunter with less than stellar results to find replacement managers in Midland, I decided to take on this task personally. It was 1976, and it seemed appropriate to spend a little time with my other properties out West as well. So my family and I picked up and moved to Santa Fe for a few months.

Within a month or so, I found the kind of manager I was looking for to operate the Inn of the Governors. He was a lieutenant colonel, just retired from the air force, named Ed Sweeney. Ed had lived in Santa Fe earlier, wanted to come back permanently, and was well connected around town. While he had no hotel experience, he was an obvious "people person." I felt he would learn the ropes of operating a hotel quickly enough to make up for his lack of experience. As it turned out, he not only met my performance expectations but also remained our manager for over thirteen years.

The Competition in Downtown Santa Fe

A couple of years before Ed took over, two new upscale hotels had been built close to our location. One was a 160-room Hilton, the other a 135-room independent hotel named the Inn at Loretto. It later became the flagship property of a small upscale chain. These two new hotels were soon joined by a third property, a more-distant 120-room Sheraton.

Together, these three new properties produced a glut of hotel rooms in the downtown area. In the year following their completion, the operating profit at our Inn fell to its lowest point ever—$55,000. It was just enough to service our modest mortgage.

Within a short period, all three of the new properties were in trouble. The Hilton and Sheraton wound up in bankruptcy, while the Inn at Loretto fared a little better because of an owner with deep pockets.

In such a market, our new manager, Ed Sweeney, had his work cut out.

By the mid-1980s, the Sheraton, after more than one ownership and name change, still had problems, but the Hilton and the Inn at Loretto were at least on their feet. Then came two more higher-end hotels. The first was the very luxurious Inn of the Anasazi, developed by a former top executive of Rosewood Properties. The other was the 212-room Eldorado, sponsored by William Zeckendorf Jr. The Anasazi quickly became Santa Fe's carriage-trade hotel. The Eldorado dazzled me with its reported cost. The average room rate that would be needed to service the reported mortgage was something else.

The reported construction cost of the Eldorado was about $150,000 per room. The room rate needed to support such a cost was about double the average rate at the Inn at Loretto, which, prior to these two new properties, had the highest rates in the downtown area. Based on the numbers I was hearing, I estimated it would take the Eldorado about ten years of demand growth and 100 percent inflation before it would yield any cash flow. It looked like a doomsday scenario. But, rather quickly, things changed.

Santa Fe: A National and International Tourist Destination

I never met Bill Zeckendorf Jr. and was never privy to just what went on after the Eldorado opened. But I surmise the following from reports around town. The hotel failed to generate the income stream needed to service its debt and reverted to some degree of control by the lender. At the same time, something—maybe mere chance or maybe someone like Bill Zeckendorf—started giving Santa Fe a major push. All at once, the town started getting publicity like never before. It began slowly in magazines and newspapers and seemed to become contagious. Before long, there was Santa Fe "style," Santa Fe this, Santa Fe that. Next thing you knew, it was showing up in the top one, two or three of our nation's most desirable tourist destinations.

Santa Fe had arrived. In a remarkably short time, it had gone from a regional to a national and even international tourist destination.

That transformation cut two ways in the downtown Santa Fe hotel market. This second wave of hotel construction increased available rooms by about 20 percent. But offsetting this was the wider recognition of Santa Fe as a destination. And, over time, this led to healthy increases in both real estate values and hotel room rates in the downtown area.

Meanwhile, Back at the Inn of the Governors

While Santa Fe was in this market transition, the Inn of the Governors was also in transition. Seeing what was coming, we added twenty upscale rooms in what we named the Governors' Wing. It cost roughly $55,000 per room versus about $9,000 each for the original eighty rooms. With this addition, the inn's net annual operating profit quickly rose about one-third, from around $300,000 to about $400,000—only a hint of things to come.

The second transition at the Inn was to a new general manager. Ed Sweeney had indicated in 1987 a wish to retire and had been training his successor, Charlotte Sliva, for some time. Charlotte, whose background was impressive, had managed the Inn at Loretto at one point and then a large hotel in Boston. Word was out she wanted to return to Santa Fe.

I had her come to Florida, where I was living at the time, to be interviewed over a long lunch at a hotel near the airport. Our discussion focused mostly on taking the Inn of the Governors to the next level. When I found that her thinking about what was needed mirrored mine almost exactly, I hired her on the spot. She turned out to be a great manager and remained at the Inn until she retired more than fifteen years later.

Measuring Comparative Hotel Performance in Downtown Santa Fe

Going back to at least the 1970s, the Rocky Mountain Lodging Association has published each month, as well as annually, the average occupancy and room rate for virtually all of Santa Fe's downtown hotels.

Multiplying any hotel's average occupancy by its average room rate yields what is termed its revpar or revenue-per-available-room. A relatively high revpar usually indicates high profitability. Because the association publishes every month the average revpar of Santa Fe's downtown hotels, it is possible to see how you are doing versus your immediate competitor. This gives each operator a precise ongoing measurement of his or her relative revenue performance. It is not only easy to see how your hotel is doing versus the pack but, most important, whether your performance is improving or declining.

After the second and most recent wave of post-1970 room additions in downtown Santa Fe, which featured not only the Anasazi and Eldorado but several other additions of ten to sixty rooms, the Inn of the Governors's annual revpar stayed rather consistently around 90 percent of the downtown average. That was in the late 1980s and early 1990s. It was not until the mid-1990s that we executed the first major change in our management system and initiated a climb in our relative performance.

That change was to adopt the basic management philosophy of W. Edwards Deming, the same philosophy that powered the success of Toyota and other Japanese exporters after World War II. Deming's ideas start with the premise that you always need to keep in mind you are in business, first and foremost, to serve your customers. So you need to focus on continual quality improvement of your products and services, putting customer satisfaction and delight ahead of quarterly profits. That is how you create loyal customers and ensure that long-term profitability will more than take care of itself.

That focus brings a third party, the customer, into your relationship with your employees and helps soften the idea that owners and managers are out only for themselves. Customer satisfaction creates a goal on which both labor and management can agree. Deming, being merely a consultant to big business rather than an owner, had a limited influence on his client-owners profit-sharing policies. He did encourage them to engage in profit sharing, but none of the plans with which I am familiar came close to the 60–80 percent of expanding profits being paid out by Lincoln and Nucor. For our part, we started paying out monthly bonuses amounting to 30 percent of any and all profit gains over the same year-earlier month.

In retrospect, we found the adoption of Deming's ideas an excellent lead into a Lincoln-type system, but we found it took us only about halfway across the traditional divide between win-lose and win-win management. My experience to date tells me that, at least in a service business, it is better to make the jump all the way across and count on your employees to help you over the bumps.

By 2004, the Inn's revpar had reached just over 100 percent of the downtown average. Every employee was receiving monthly bonuses of about $80 a month—roughly $1,000 annually. It was obviously progress, but I felt we still had plenty of untapped upside potential. So I went back to the drawing board to further refine our profit-sharing plan. That's when I began to reconsider Lincoln's approach.

As earlier mentioned, I had read about Lincoln's remarkable success and had been fortunate enough to discuss his ideas with him before getting into business on my own. When I later got into my first reasonably stable operating business, our hotel in Midland, Texas, I was as afflicted as others with the belief that the system Lincoln had developed in manufacturing would never work in a service business.

Only after years of pursuing Deming's ideas did I read in detail what Nucor had been up to and how they were about to become America's largest steel producer. While they, like Lincoln, were still awarding bonuses based on tangible measurements of productivity when and where appropriate, they were doing so on a team basis. That provided the first insight that using team performance to measure the productivity of one's employees might just work in service businesses.

That was late 2002, following the dot-com bust and the recession occasioned by 9/11. After these downturns, I decided to maintain the bonuses to all of our employees at a $1,000 annual rate, about the amount they had reached just before the economy went sour. Maintaining that bonus, however, was not totally positive. I could see that some of the staff had started to regard the $1,000 as an entitlement, which was the last thing I had in mind.

- By late 2004, I decided to pull out the stops. So I raised the employees' share of expanding profits from 30 percent to 70 percent, roughly the same percentage used by Lincoln and Nucor. While I would not describe what followed, which was partially aided by an improving economy, as an immediate explosion, in less than four years, we experienced these major changes at the Inn of the Governors: Our revpar rose from just over 100 percent to 137 percent of the downtown average. Individual bonuses reached an annual rate of over $8,000. The hotel's net operating profit, which was close to an already formidable level of $1.8 million, increased to over $3 million just before the 2008 recession settled in. The return to the Inn's owners before that event, which included adjustments for inflation of about $200,000, rose from about $1.8 million to about $2.3 million.

By then, as the majority owner, I was reminded of a page in the *New York Times* the day after Frank Sinatra died. It had been taken out by General Motors. Just above a vintage Cadillac convertible with its headlights colored to look like blue eyes, the caption read, "Thanks for the Ride!"

I felt a need to send the same happy message to my staff at the Inn.

CHAPTER 4

Service Businesses: the Low-Hanging Fruit on the Road to the WWEW

All Those Others Who Failed to Follow Lincoln

Seeing the remarkable growth in productivity and market share Lincoln Electric had achieved in six-plus years, why didn't other manufacturers rush to adopt its clearly superior workplace model?

A parallel question might be: why didn't Bethlehem Steel and other big steel producers, upon seeing how Nucor employees were becoming vastly more productive than their own, alter course and reverse what became their death marches?

The seeming answer to both questions is much the same as why most couples headed for divorce court can't put humpty dumpty back together. Disaffection and lack of trust between the partners, like that between labor and management, had become so entrenched that the task of reversing it seemed too difficult to pursue.

The broader question is why successful manufacturers who might have duplicated Lincoln's extraordinary success in their own fields exhibited little interest in doing so. The answer seems to have involved both hardened attitudes and the relatively slow feedback loops inherent in manufacturing. What is now apparent—"the pity of it all" from a systems standpoint—is this: first, the fast-expanding profits that resulted from higher employee productivity at Lincoln would never have come into being without its generous bonus system, which sparked that productivity and those profits. Second and equally apparent is that, in addition to these tangible benefits the system created, intangible benefits were sacrificed that were arguably of equal or even greater value.

Low-Hanging Fruit

If you've ever tried to pick fruit from an apple tree, you know that the easiest apples to reach are on the low-hanging branches. You simply walk up to the tree and look for the apple you want and reach for it. If what you want is on a higher branch, the job, which likely requires a ladder, is a lot harder. So if you're hungry, you'll pick what is easy to reach.

When you look at most American work organizations as possible candidates for a "workplace where everyone wins," you conclude that long-unionized companies with limiting work rules are not the low-hanging fruit you want to pick first. Their fruit is among the hardest to reach. Only when market forces demand it or a critical mass of both owners and workers have discovered the benefits of win-win management and are shouting, "What are the rest of you waiting for?" are these difficult candidates likely to change their ways and join the parade. Even then, some of them will be so stuck in their ways, they'll probably end up like Big Steel—choosing bankruptcy over change.

Four Reasons the Service Sector Provides the Low-Hanging Fruit

There are four easily identifiable reasons why service businesses are the best candidates for relatively rapid and easy implementation of a WWEW.

First, fast feedback from end customers help define those service businesses where the lowest-hanging fruit of the WWEW are found. In fact, fast feedback loops are the main factor between the ease of implementing a WWEW in a service business and the difficulty of such implementation in manufacturing. As used here, the term *fast feedback loops* marks the speed of getting products and/or services to the customer and the speed of customer response.

For example, each customer in a restaurant receiving much better than normal food and service can return for dinner the same night and, perhaps, once again the same week. Multiply that by many delighted returning customers over a month, and it amounts to a significant increase in normal business volume. By the tenth of the following month, the manager can readily determine the profit increase over the same year-earlier month and pay out a large part of the increase to those responsible—the employees.

A simple example of the difference in feedback speed is product improvement For manufacturers, the design and testing of a new product can take from months to years. For a restaurant, it can happen between lunch and dinner.

The second reason the low-hanging fruit of the WWEW is found in the service sector is that most service businesses are small and local, allowing an ease of communication from top to bottom. Most of the staff know each other, which facilitates the process by which workers can become comfortably assimilated as partners into a WWEW. The third reason is that service employees tend to be younger, less set in their ways, less unionized and more adaptable than manufacturing employees.

The fourth reason is the difference in the nature of a service business from manufacturing. Efficiency in service is involved, largely with creating positive people-connections that foster mutual likeability or interpersonal "glue." This leads to easy communication and growing rapport. A well-trained and highly motivated staff can quickly create such rapport among both staff and customers.

In total contrast, manufacturing is primarily concerned with producing tangible products, which are dependent on time, often a lot more time than sometimes necessary. One reason is the lack of direct contact with end customers.

Which brings us to the single overriding issue that interacts with all four of the above reasons: trust.

The WWEW and Trust

If and when the WWEW becomes a broadly used and well-recognized way of organizing the workplace—a status it has yet to achieve—implementing a WWEW, even in manufacturing, could be fairly simple. Workers would soon see that others, working for a competitor organized as a WWEW, enjoy a much better deal than they have. They would be eager to enjoy benefits from the same deal. That is why whenever Nucor opened new plants, thousands of people lined up wanting to work for them.

But, as we know, Lincoln and Nucor are the exceptions, not the rule. Absent knowledge of the potential benefits of the WWEW, workers in a traditional win-lose manufacturing organization are likely to be suspicious of a new approach because many have a built-in lack of trust in the motives of company management. If offered 70 percent of expanding earnings for working more productively, the understandable reaction would likely be, "What kind of wool is management trying to pull over our eyes this time?" This mistrust helps explain why, on the one hand, Lincoln's approach never gained the support of owners or workers in manufacturing elsewhere. On the other hand, already-successful manufacturers, aware of labor's limited trust, have, as noted, understandably concluded about their own organizations: "If it ain't broke, don't fix it."

The major exceptions to this standoff seem to be the few organizations noted herein, where either employee jobs were at risk or the company was a worker-friendly start-up where work standards were yet to be developed. Even these few cases needed unusual leaders who saw the need for trust as the basis for real win-win cooperation.

This sensitivity in traditional organizations to the issue of trust changes radically when a work organization, such as a table-service restaurant, can generate bonuses not in a year but in a month. Their employees also soon realize they are part of a company culture infinitely more positive than anything they may have experienced before.

A Clear Alternative

These positive potentials of the WWEW frame an obvious alternative to the negative feelings and relationships so common in today's workplace. One observer describing the traditional workplace noted, "Most people choose their employer because they like the company and leave because of growing dislike for their supervisor."

As positive people-potentials are tapped, a WWEW's culture quickly progresses well beyond anything possible in traditional businesses. This is because the atmosphere created by a WWEW, as we have witnessed in our two service organizations, transcends both the disaffection and the fear so common in a win-lose workplace. In addition, the cross-purposes between labor and management in such traditional workplaces serve to block potentials to radically improve the quality of life for all concerned.

Thus, can we all take heart from what is implied by the recent success of our two WWEWs from among the low-hanging fruit in the service sector. They reflect the potential for a long-overdue spread of the higher workplace system first fashioned at Lincoln Electric. As it spreads, it will hopefully start to reverse the negative trends afflicting our nation.

One bright light in this picture deserves everyone's attention. In what seems a Lincoln-like reaction to current hard times, Bob King, president of the United Automobile Workers, recently announced that his union has shifted from confrontation to cooperation with management. Sounds wonderful. Let's hope it can last and that he will become a real trailblazer in bridging the traditional divide between labor and management in manufacturing.

CHAPTER 5

A Much-Delayed Second Success: the Waterway Cafe

An Unexpected Development

After enjoying success with managing the Sheraton Inn in Midland and the Inn of the Governors in Santa Fe, I expected my business focus to center entirely on my operations in the Southwest. Little did I suspect that in a few years, I would find myself owning a large restaurant in South Florida. But that's what happened, and here's how it came about.

During the 1970s, Midland, Texas, had an up-and-down economy, largely the consequence of Middle East oil embargoes. By 1980, as the result of the late-1970s embargo, Midland was once again an oil boomtown. All of the major oil companies were expanding operations there, and more high-rise office buildings were going up. Our Sheraton Inn was diagonally across an intersection from Midland's tallest office building, the twenty-seven-story First National Bank of Midland. Because of the oil resources nearby, the bank was one of the five largest independent banks west of the Mississippi.

In the heady days of an earlier oil boom, Midland had adopted the slogan, "The sky's the limit in Midland, Texas." That slogan reached what seemed its zenith in the 1980 boom when the First National Bank announced a landmark project. It had assembled a superblock of property immediately south of its existing location and was planning to build three forty-story office buildings on this superblock. The first tower was to be directly across the street from the entrance to our Sheraton Inn, which occupied most of its own block.

We had already received inquiries from several potential buyers of the Sheraton when a representative of Shell Oil called. He indicated his firm's interest in acquiring the two-story Sheraton and replacing it with a high-rise office building. When I told him what the Sheraton was worth as a hotel, however, he quickly figured what that would equate to as a land cost per square foot. He explained that amount was substantially higher than what they had paid for a comparable site in Tulsa, Oklahoma, a much larger city. End of conversation.

About a month later, I had a call from a junior partner in the Sheraton who was a close friend and partner with me in other projects. He allowed a friend, who wished to remain unidentified, who wanted to buy the Sheraton and build a major office building there. Since I was not really interested in selling the property, I described my discussion with the Shell representative, cited the numbers involved, and suggested this new party would likely have the same negative reaction.

To my surprise, a message came back within twenty-four hours that this new party would pay half again the amount Shell had considered excessive. He further instructed my friend to say to me, "If you won't take that, tell him what will you take?" I raised his offer by another 50 percent. He accepted, and within a day, I received a letter of credit for 10 percent of the purchase price. We closed the sale for cash sixty days later.

It turned out the buyer was planning to buy the block south of the Sheraton as well. He wanted to build a fifty-four-story obelisk on the Sheraton site and a round parking garage across the street on the block south. They would be connected by an enclosed walkway and configured so the completed project would resemble a huge oilrig with an attached storage tank.

Unfortunately, the 1980 oil boom quickly went bust, as did the First National Bank and its plans for three forty-story office buildings. The new owner of the Sheraton, not anticipating what was coming, quickly razed the hotel to make a statement. The loss of the still-popular pub, never to return, was mourned by many. The last time I was in Midland, the site of the one-time Sheraton was an underutilized parking lot.

That sale illustrates how wild real estate can get in such circumstances and how, once again, luck had smiled on me. It also set the stage for the development of a second WWEW; this one turned out to be a large waterfront restaurant ten miles north of Palm Beach, Florida.

The Change in Plans

At the time of the Sheraton sale, my family and I were spending our winters in Florida and summers in New England. The sale left me with more cash than usual, burning a hole in my pocket. So I decided to build a hotel in Florida to replace the one I had just sold.

I started considering designs and looking around for suitable locations. What I soon found was that most of the existing hotels in the area were not doing that well, and still more hotels were either under construction or on the drawing boards. One day, during a discussion of this situation with a realtor friend, he "confided" that the only kind of project that could provide an immediate cash flow in our area was a restaurant on the Intracoastal Waterway. And it just so happened that he had an option on the perfect site.

I took his sales pitch with a grain of salt but looked at the property anyway. At the time, it was a working boatyard that abutted the bridge over the Intracoastal Waterway on PGA Boulevard, a largely undeveloped, east-west thoroughfare in the city of Palm Beach Gardens. Most of the undeveloped property nearby was still pastureland. It had been assembled by John D. MacArthur, founder of the Chicago-based MacArthur Foundation. With big plans for the area, MacArthur had induced the Professional Golfers Association (PGA) to build its headquarters and several golf courses about three miles west of the site on which my realtor friend held his option.

I felt this site—only 1.2 acres—was too small for what I might like to do, so I told my friend if he could secure options on five adjoining homes, I would be interested. He did secure the options at a reasonable price, and I subsequently bought the property.

The Waterway Café

The restaurant that I named the Waterway Cafe opened in April 1986. It was large and quite open. I had told the architect to design it as F. Scott Fitzgerald might have liked, as a party pavilion on the waterway. The seating was arranged on three levels to allow all of the customers to watch the boats going by. The structure had three hundred seats indoors and another one hundred outside. Half of the latter were on a floating bar at the end of the former marina's travel lift.

My realtor friend was so enthusiastic about the project, he became a partner in the deal. Unhappily, the restaurant lost money for the first couple of years, which discouraged him. So he asked me to buy him out, which I did.

Within three years after the Waterway's opening, two important things occurred in the area. In late 1988, the MacArthur Foundation released enough land one mile west of our site for the development of the upscale Gardens Mall—then to be Florida's largest mall, with 1.3 million square feet of retail space. It had all of the top names.

At about the same time, another mile west, Interstate 95 was extended up from West Palm Beach to PGA Boulevard. Our potential customer base suddenly grew significantly.

In 1995, when we were introducing Deming's management ideas at the Inn of the Governors in Santa Fe, I decided to do the same at the Waterway Cafe. By then, our sales at the Waterway had reached about $4 million annually, with net operating profit of roughly $600,000. I was glad to have a second somewhat different kind of business where I could apply Deming's philosophy simultaneously. The management systems at the Inn in Santa Fe and the Waterway Cafe could evolve together. I expected each could learn from the other.

During the years up to 2004, while Deming's ideas were elevating, our revenue per available room at the Inn of the Governors from 85–90 percent of the downtown Santa Fe average to just over

100 percent, our annual net operating profit at the Waterway was rising to about $800,000. All things considered, both businesses were making good progress. At both locations, 30 percent of expanding earnings were being distributed equally to all employees.

Unfortunately, the recession following 9/11 produced a significant soft patch. The bonuses, which had reached an annual rate of over $1,000 for every employee at both locations, began to stagnate a bit. So I decided—as a matter of good faith and confidence in our employees—not to let it drop below the $1,000 rate. Soon, however, it appeared that maintaining the bonus at $1,000 was taking some steam out of the program. The regular monthly checks started to be viewed as more of an entitlement than an incentive.

Accelerated Improvement

When I pulled out the stops and increased the bonus at the Inn of the Governors to 70 percent of expanding profits versus the 30 percent being paid out at the time, it definitely kick-started a major improvement in sales and net operating profit. So I decided to offer the same 70 percent to our staff at the Waterway Cafe.

A most notable difference between the two properties came after this shift to 70 percent at the Waterway. In little over a year, sales there increased to over $6 million, and the annual individual bonus rate rose to $3,500. That was about $500 higher than the then-rate at the Inn. This gave us the first indicator that a casual-dining restaurant enjoyed a potential to elevate sales and earnings a bit faster than a hotel. This seemed logical enough to make me think we might be seeing sales at the Waterway in the range of $10 million in three to four years, and an annual bonus rate in the $10–12,000 range. But then the wheels began to fall off.

Our first taste of adversity came with the state's decision to rebuild the bridge adjoining the Waterway Cafe's site. We knew it was coming, but we did not anticipate the duration or extent of the damage to our sales and profits. Six traffic lanes were permanently reduced to two—sometimes none—for two-plus years. Customers started avoiding the bridge—and us—due to traffic delays. The name

PGA came to mean "Please Go Around." Our sales, which had been increasing by over 10 percent a year were suddenly down 15 percent.

At about the same time the bridge-rebuilding project began, the MacArthur Foundation decided to release all of its vacant commercial land between our site and the PGA development three miles west of us. This land had been held off the market far longer than normal. As soon as it was released, it created what seemed a great sucking sound, pulling commercial developers from every direction into the area all at once. Their attitude, suggested by a newspaper article, seemed to be "build it, and they will come." Five new satellite centers opened one after the other with combined retail space approaching that of the Gardens Mall.

All of these new projects came on line about the time the bridge project adjoining our site was completed. The number of restaurants between our site and the PGA development, some of which had sponsors as distant as Los Angeles and New York, had grown from twenty-one to over ninety, inspiring an article in the *Palm Beach Post* titled, "Eat Your Way Down PGA Boulevard."

Such a glut of new competition was our second hit to what seemed like a highly positive growth potential. When I purchased, the Waterway site had become, for the immediate period ahead at least, an area overwhelmed by an excess of restaurants. It was late 2007, and we now had, almost next door, Friday's, Chili's, a Cheesecake Factory, the Capital Grill, and on and on and on. You name it, and we had it—plus a significant number of good small operators.

Thanks to the WWEW we had going at the Waterway Cafe, we fared better than might have been expected. Our sales, which had dropped from over $6.2 million to $5.3 million while the bridge was being rebuilt, actually climbed back to $6.2 million during the year after completion of the bridge project—despite the hordes of new competition. But then came our third "hit," the Great Recession, which arrived for us in August 2008.

Over the next two years, the Waterway's annual sales declined from $6.2 million until they began to stabilize at around $5.7 million. New home construction in the area, which topped out in 2006–07, had come to a standstill. WCI, the national developer that kicked off the building boom in the area, was out of business. Several national home-builders, such as Toll Brothers, Hovnanian, and Centex shut down and/or cancelled all of their projects nearby. Three retail centers totaling about seven hundred thousand square feet declared bankruptcy. Of the seventy new restaurants, most of the large-chain properties hung on as the independent operators suffered the most failures. The weeding-out process continues.

The Waterway Cafe finished 2009 with sales of $6 million and a net operating profit of $835,000. Based on my earlier projection of annual sales of $10 million, that looked like a major failure. Compared with the bloodletting among the other restaurants on PGA Boulevard, however, it seemed a great success. What carried the day? It was a combination of the loyalty of our very-low-turnover staff as well as the loyalty they had created among the area's customer base.

In late 2010, we added some additional outside seating on vacant ground adjoining our original building. Even though it was a low-budget project, its format, which copied the high-value approach used at the Inn of the Governors' restaurant, soon led to the Waterway Cafe reaching its highest weekly sales ever. With the peak of the winter season still ahead, our earlier projections of $10 million in annual sales and average annual bonuses of $10–12,000 per staff member began to look achievable once again.

CHAPTER 6

The Four Drivers of the WWEW

For those considering implementation of the WWEW, the following are its four main elements or "drivers":

1. a team focus on the customer,
2. partner-size gainsharing,
3. a three-part performance-tracking system, and
4. life skills training.

The First Driver: a Team Focus on the Customer

In the late 1940s, W. Edwards Deming developed a new and very successful management system that transformed Japanese automobile companies, electronics manufacturers, and others into major world players. Yet it took another three-plus decades (and a TV documentary titled *If Japan Can, Why Can't We?*) before American business started connecting the dots between what Deming, an American, started teaching Japanese manufacturers soon after World War II and how, by 1980, these Japanese manufacturers had become so influential—in many cases dominant—in various American industries.

Deming focused his attention on labor and management cooperating to build customer satisfaction and delight through continual improvement of products and services.

To grasp Deming's influence, one need only read the words of Shoichiro Toyoda, president of the Toyota Motor Corporation, at the presentation in 1991 of Japan's Deming Prize: "There is not a day I don't think about what Dr. Deming meant to us. Deming is the core of our management."

In many ways, James Lincoln was already practicing the customer focus Deming later started teaching in Japan. Yet, there is no evidence that either man related his approach to that of the other. Nor is there much to suggest that Nucor or Worthington Industries related their approaches to Lincoln's, Deming's, or each other's. There is one book titled *Lasting Value, Lessons from a Century of Agility at Lincoln Electric* that compares the systems and performance of Lincoln, Nucor, and Worthington. There is little to suggest anywhere, however, the point made here that these three companies deserve to be recognized as pioneers of a new and higher workplace system. And, like Deming's, it puts customer satisfaction first and lets the "bottom line" take care of itself.

Important to remember is that Deming was a consultant, not a business owner. Few of the companies he advised established profit-sharing plans that approached the percentage of increasing profits distributed to their employees by Lincoln, Nucor, and Worthington.

Compared to the WWEW, this lack of partner-like profit sharing renders Deming's approach less than complete, as described in driver number 2: partner-size gainsharing. Despite this limitation, Deming's approach has enjoyed major successes, especially in Japan, and through many books, his system has been well-explained.

Two of the best books about Deming and his approach are *Quality or Else* by Clare Crawford-Mason and Lloyd Dobyns, and Mary Walton's, *The Deming Management Method*. The former gave rise to a PBS series of the same name and, thereafter, *The Deming Video Library*.

The Second Driver: Partner-Size Gainsharing

John McConnell, a coal miner's son and the first in his family to ever attend college, was the founder and, for over half a century, the man in charge of Worthington Industries, a manufacturer of steel parts and panels. Just before he died in 2008, McConnell's publicly held company he founded in 1955 with a $600 loan on his Oldsmobile, enjoyed a market capitalization of about $2 billion.

At a meeting of manufacturers where McConnell described Worthington's management system, a young and eager attendee sought him out after the meeting. He wanted to install Worthington's system in his own company and needed more detail. So they talked for the better part of an hour. At the end of their conversation, McConnell reemphasized a point he had made more than once: that a major share of expanding profits should be distributed to the employees. This was the key to creating these profits.

At the same gathering a year later, the two men met again, and McConnell asked the young man how his program had worked out. The chap stammered a bit and said, "Not too well." When asked if he had adopted Worthington's bonus system, the answer was, "We just couldn't do that."

In retrospect, given the slow feedback loops inherent in manufacturing and the lack of trust that usually exists between labor and management under traditional capitalism, what the young man reported back to Mr. McConnell should not have been that much of a surprise.

Even in service businesses where fast feedback loops can transcend the trust issue through rapid results, owners can be sufficiently stuck in the fixed-pie syndrome; they may have trouble realizing a point win-win organizations like Lincoln, Nucor, and Worthington understood from the beginning: unless a major share of earnings increases are paid out to the people doing the work, these increases, absent chance factors, will not come into being.

Nor would the remaining share going to the owners come into being. Nor would the major reductions in supervisory costs nor the low rates of staff turnover nor the countless intangible benefits of their systems be realized.

In our two service-sector WWEWs, we have in the past started each year by adjusting the baseline above, which the gainsharing payouts apply to reflect the effect of inflation on the owners' investment. Under consideration now is giving our staffs more protection against extraordinary changes in market conditions that diminish their bonus potential. Nucor's Ken Iverson, operating in an industry more subject than most to extraordinary changes in market demand, used a system he called pain-sharing. As for Lincoln, when excessively rapid global expansion resulted in operating losses, the company actually borrowed money from their bank to fund bonuses.

For good reason, we look at and treat all of our staff members as operating partners. While they have no investment in or claim on either the assets or appreciation of the business's value, they have—and deserve—the largest share of those expanding short-term profits for which they are, in virtually all cases, responsible.

This recognition of partnership helps nurture among staff members the feelings of shared purpose with the owners that keep alive their commitment to continual improvement of products and services and all that implies. This sense of partnership also powers the many intangible benefits that flow from the WWEW.

Once owners have qualified their businesses as suitable to become WWEWs, they need to recognize they are entering into a covenant with their staffs, both frontline workers and supervisors. In this covenant, they are trading the major share of increases in short-term earnings, no matter what their source, for an entirely new kind of business organization. It operates a win-win system that, by transcending the disaffection, cross-purposes and related conflicts of win-lose organizations, actually creates these earnings increases in virtually all cases. It also nurtures the ever-greater trust, respect, and cooperation of employees who drives their improving productivity and performance—and the other increasingly positive outcomes all business owner would love to have but few enjoy. During any moment of doubt, it is helpful for an owner to revisit the earlier description of the outcomes that followed Lincoln's uncompromising commitment to their employees.

The Third Driver: a Three-Part Performance Tracking System

This system was inspired by the time-honored adage, "What gets measured is what gets done" or, conversely, "What doesn't get measured is likely not to get done." So our WWEWs are guided by an information system more capable than most of helping continual drive performance improvement.

The first part of this system involves tracking both same-month figures and trailing-twelve-month trends taken from our monthly operating statements (see Appendix A). This tracking covers all income and expense items considered noteworthy and goes back several years.

The second part of the system reports comments of in-house sources: customers, employees, and suppliers.

The third part involves relevant comments and ratings from online reviews of our performance. The major rating firms are Trip Advisor, Yelp, and Yahoo. They are generally reliable providers of hotel and restaurant ratings that are read by many potential customers. Happily, our WWEWs consistently rate near the top—not infrequently at the top—of like properties in their respective markets.

Information from these sources is used to guide efforts to continually improve our products and services. This approach, besides driving performance gains, helps build bonds between staff members.

The information gathered from these diverse sources is made available to all employees. One bonus is that, as frontline staff members become more familiar with the tracking of operating data and related comments, increased feelings of ownership and empowerment naturally follow.

The Fourth Driver: Life Skills Training

Companies organized as WWEWs can benefit enormously from staffs possessing the skills to connect quickly, positively, and permanently with other people, both customers and fellow staff members; organize goals and priorities—short-term, midterm and long-term; frame most problems not as single events but as signals of opportunity to improve the systems in which they arose; frame most issues and events not in isolation but as systems issues and events.

A WWEW places high value on training all staff members to develop and continually improve these life skills and use them not only with customers but other staff members as well. Moreover, these skills enhance the effectiveness of staff members, not only on the job but off the job, and not only in their present positions but any future positions.

Training in these skills takes a number of forms, such as booklets and papers addressing key points of each skill, brief reviews of these points during team meetings and, not least, online backups.

CHAPTER 7

The Benefits of the WWEW: Tangible and Intangible

For any business owner, making—or even considering—the move from traditional win-lose capitalism to a WWEW requires a major mind-set shift. Without total grasp of the benefits of the WWEW and the polar difference between these two approaches, few owners are likely to enjoy an easy transition. Even a review of the wonderful transformation that occurred at Lincoln Electric upon its decision to share with its employees the major part of expanding profits may not sweep away an owner's time-conditioned doubts. Nor is it easy for an owner, before making this transition, to realize that the long-term benefits of a WWEW outweigh many times over the distributions of expanding profits made to the employees.

In those cases where transitioning to a WWEW is currently practical, it is essential to realize that the benefits going to the owner, tangible and intangible, short-term and long-term, can and should also outweigh many times over what the owner might initially perceive as giving up or relinquishing a certain amount of financial gain.

Building Trust with Staff

Successful implementation of a WWEW depends on how owners communicate with their staffs. Staff members need to understand the benefits available to them and, most important, need to have full trust that the owner will stay the course. Since the very idea of a WWEW will be surprisingly new to staff members, establishing this recognition and trust poses a significant challenge for most businesses. The problem begins with the fact that a win-lose relationships between labor and management may well have left long-embedded mistrust in employee attitudes and expectations.

Fortunately, most service businesses, given their rapid feedback loops, can put gainsharings in the pockets of frontline staff members quickly enough to defuse the lack of trust issue. Such businesses qualify as the "low-hanging fruit" of the WWEW. These businesses enjoy direct contact between staff members and end customers and rapid customer feedback. These two circumstances allow staff members in these businesses to quickly turn customer satisfaction and delight into repeat business, to make real-time product improvements, to solve problems without delay, and to quickly generate significant gainsharings for themselves. Casual table-service restaurants are, perhaps, the best example of such businesses.

Picking this low-hanging fruit first—getting various businesses to try a WWEW—is key to spreading knowledge of its benefits throughout ever-growing numbers of both owners and employees. Until knowledge of how a WWEW can transform a business becomes fairly widespread, installing a WWEW in any business will involve some element of pioneering.

Appropriate to note is that it was a manufacturing firm, Lincoln Electric, that, with a sizeable number of employees, established the first large model of a truly win-win system of management. However, Lincoln enjoyed an advantage shared by few other manufacturers—a high level of trust already in place among most employees. This appears to have resulted from the long-standing functioning of the company's advisory board, a group that included both workers and managers. Also, the company's success was likely aided by the concern about job losses faced by many manufacturing employees during the Great Depression.

The Many Benefits of the WWEW

When implementing WWEWs in our two service businesses, we were fortunate to enjoy great success in a short period of time. While adjusting to the worst economic times since the Great Depression, we have well exceeded and expected to continue exceeding the performance of our competitors. It is important to remember that we are in the kind of businesses—restaurants and hotels—where the potential for large profit gains at the expense of competitors is not common. Only committed ownership and highly motivated staffs could have made happen the kind of improvements in quality of service and products that lets us continue exceeding the performance of our competitors.

Many of the benefits of the WWEW are simply the reciprocals of the problems afflicting traditional win-lose management as cited in chapter 1. These afflictions are worth revisiting given this insight. In summary, their reciprocity creates a climate in a WWEW that is as different as day and night from today's win-lose norm. In addition, there are some subtleties involved with the WWEW's tangible benefits that deserve special mention.

More About the Tangible Benefits

- The earnings increases distributed to the working staff. These distributions to all of our employees are the engine that drives out WWEWs and guarantee that they remain workplaces where everyone wins. In the process, these gainsharings also create a unity of purpose and feeling of partnership among all employees that totally differentiate the WWEW from the traditional win-lose style of capitalism.

Just as the engine that drives an automobile produces both direct and indirect outcomes, this gainsharing commitment drives both the tangible and intangible benefits of the WWEW. Compared to the traditional style of managing, which is well-recognized as a source of cross-purposes and disaffection between labor and management, the WWEW achieves exactly the opposite. The value of the

WWEW's ability to transform competition into cooperation among all of the individuals involved—owners, managers, and frontline workers—cannot be overstated. And while any WWEW may need a little adjusting now and then, it is nothing short of a magnificent business machine that can fly circles around its competitors.

- The earnings increases distributed to the owners. Although these distributions may at first seem less than impressive, the potential long-term benefits that can accrue to the owners go far beyond what first appearances may suggest. These benefits start with the fact that, as a result of being awarded the major share of increased profits, the staff members bestow on the owners the magnificent business machine just described. This machine is capable of creating radically better performance than its competitors. And, with such a machine, the owners can leverage great long-term benefits.

- For example, this magnificent machine will generate simultaneously growing market share for the business and lower prices for the customer. Both will fuel further expansion of the business. Often, this expansion can be financed internally out of profits. If and when it is appropriate to seek outside financing from banks, venture capital groups or a public offering of shares in the company, it can likely be arranged with relative ease, given the high-performance capabilities of the WWEW.

- Very low staff turnover. This is one of the major early benefits flowing from an owner's financial commitment to the working staff. Not only are the cost and time requirements of hiring and training new employees drastically reduced—as is the time needed for new employees to get up to speed—but all kinds of related adjustments are equally diminished.

The loss of one staff member and the hiring of a replacement is not unlike having a death in the family and the arrival of a new baby at the same time. Other staff members have to adjust, and if the employee you lost was a good one, customers may be lost as well.

Staff turnover at both of our properties is only a small fraction of the norm for restaurants and hotels. As a result, we have not had to advertise for help in years. We maintain lists of highly qualified prospects wanting to join the family. Many have been recommended by existing staff members. Further, more often than not, good employees lured away by other employers in the area tend to return before long, asking for their old jobs back.

- Less need for supervision. When staff members are motivated to do things right and cooperate with fellow employees, all kinds of good things happen. Not the least is that managers can focus more on improving products and services and very little on putting out fires. In many cases, the need for supervision can be totally eliminated.

- Continually improving quality of both service and related products. Another key benefit of the gainsharing is the desire of all staff members to continually improve the experience of every customer. This higher quality service is what produces customers who come back again and again. And this increases not just sales, but gainsharings as well—a point not lost on the staff.

- Reduction of waste. Unlike the situation in most businesses, when staff members observe wasteful practices, instead of ignoring them and thinking, *That's the boss's problem*, they realize it's money out of their own pockets.

- Near elimination of employee abuses. Things like employee theft, absenteeism, and tardiness in getting to work tend to disappear when they have adverse effects on fellow employees. Either you're part of the team, or your fellow team members see to it that you're soon looking for employment elsewhere.

- Fewer accidents, lower insurance cost. To our surprise early on, as workman's compensation and guest liability insurance renewal dates started coming around, our premiums began declining and continued to decline until they approached minimums. Since we couldn't really explain it, we finally assigned it to the good karma of the WWEW.

- Less need for off-site supervision. Consistent with a reduced need for onsite supervision, the need for visits by offsite owners or their representatives is reduced dramatically.

More About the Intangible Benefits

As realization of the tangible benefits of the WWEW proceeds, its intangible benefits become increasingly apparent and important as the endpiece will indicate—the longer-term benefits of the WWEW are not just economic but political, social, and even philosophical. They have built-in potentials to become game changers in each of these categories. In a more immediate context, the key changes include the following:

- Replacing a top-down win-lose culture with a culture of cooperation. This shift produces positive changes almost too numerous to recite. Among the more important: bosses become more like coaches; stress and fear, commonplace under win-lose management, give way to feelings of partnership and trust; not least are the desire of the staff to be more productive generally and the opportunity to experience pride in one's work.

- A workplace climate that breeds equally numerous benefits. These include a high degree of both job and workplace stability; the near-elimination of those factors that lead to employee burnout; the too-common feeling that one's job is a burden gives way to increasing feelings that one's job can be fun; increasing awareness that most problems can be reframed as opportunities for improvement of the systems in which they developed; the appearance of totally unexpected creativity among staff members able to translate these signs of opportunity into solutions of specific problems.

Taken together, all of these benefits, tangible and intangible, define a world so different from the norm, one really needs to start experiencing it to appreciate how radically different it is. Hopefully, increasing numbers of both owners and those on the frontlines—coaching and overseeing, as well as doing the work—will start to embark upon this highly gratifying experience.

CHAPTER 8

The Challenge of Implementing a WWEW

Determining the difficulty of installing a WWEW in any specific business can be a journey into uncharted territory. While casual dining restaurants are among the best candidates for ease of implementation, manufacturers remain among the most unlikely candidates, for the same reasons that explain the failure of other manufacturers to follow Lincoln's lead back in the 1930s.

Nevertheless, certain generalizations can be made about the challenge of implementing a WWEW. First of all, businesses without enough employees to create multiple small teams are at a disadvantage. An exception can be mom-and-pop operations, some of which likely qualify unknowingly as the original WWEWs.

Second, businesses that engage heavily in speculation, like stock brokerage firms, as well as manufacturers whose products have very short life cycles, are the poorest of candidates, at least until there is a general awakening to the benefits of the WWEW.

Third, and perhaps the easiest, generalization about the challenge of installing a WWEW involves such a "general awakening" among both businesses and their employees to the tremendous potentials of the WWEW. At this time, there is virtually no awareness of these potentials. As this awareness starts to expand, so will interest in the WWEW. Ultimately, this awareness could become commonplace. At such a point, the challenge of implementing a WWEW that now exists for most companies could conceivably be swept away by a rush to create a WWEW before competitors do.

Since that happy circumstance has yet to arrive, it would be highly desirable to have an index that defines the challenge of implementing a WWEW in various business categories—in both service and manufacturing. Obviously, such an initial index would be open to expansion and refinement as experience accumulates. For now, the factors listed below seem to be the major considerations that will be involved in such an index:

- Current awareness of the benefits of the WWEW. As awareness and use of the format expands, the implementation of a WWEW—initially in service, thereafter in manufacturing—will become progressively easier. Of course, only time will tell if and when true win-win management will become the standard of business organization and usher in a new definition of what capitalism can and should be.

- Service sector versus the manufacturing sector. Until recently, the only companies of record to implement a genuine win-win style of management—Lincoln, Nucor, and Worthington Industries—have been manufacturers. The successful introduction of a WWEW in the two service businesses addressed herein—a hotel/restaurant and a large freestanding restaurant—have enlarged the frame of reference dramatically. Until now, no one seemed to believe the approach initiated by Lincoln could be implemented in service.

Long-mistaken beliefs have effectively blocked the spread of Lincoln's approach for the better part of a century and preempted the understanding that the service sector is where this approach needs to be pursued first if it is to spread through the economy. We now know that a WWEW cannot only work in the service sector but that it can be installed far more easily in service than in manufacturing.

- Speed of key feedback loops in different kinds of businesses. Do one's employees enjoy direct contact with end customers? How long does it take for a customer to express a positive experience? How long does it take for a positive experience to result in repeat business? How long does it take for a growing number of positive customer experiences to translate into higher profits and growing employee gainsharings—weeks, months, or years? How long does it take for a WWEW to develop the kind of reputation that generates rapidly increasing sales through good will?

These customer feedback loops reflect some of the key issues when implementing a WWEW in any existing business, especially one that has been operating under the traditional model of management. For a casual dining restaurant, all of these feedback loops involve outcomes favorable to a WWEW's successful implementation. On a positive implementation index of one to one hundred, where one represents the least potential for easy, successful implementation of a WWEW, and one hundred represents the best such potential, service businesses generally would score well over fifty, and most manufacturing businesses well under fifty—the latter because the feedback loops in manufacturing are so much slower than in service.

- The issue of trust between employees and management. Feedback speed is so important largely because the WWEW is a brand-new format. Its benefits are currently little understood or appreciated. This raises the issue of trust. Imagine yourself as an employee of a company with a long tradition of win-lose management. Suddenly, the company proposes (1) that labor and management engage in enthusiastic cooperation and (2) that management will give labor the largest share of increasing profits resulting from such cooperation. Can you as an employee be blamed for being skeptical and not believing what you hear? In fact, if you are a member of a labor union, such cooperation would likely violate your established work rules.

Given the degree of distrust, large or small, that may exist on the part of workers in a long-established win-lose organization, the best way to overcome this distrust is by installing WWEWs first in those companies that enjoy rapid feedback loops. These need to be sufficiently rapid to put significant gainsharings in the pockets of staff members very quickly.

To further hasten the establishment of a bridge of trust between labor and management, W. Edwards Deming's approach of making customers the third party in the labor/management relationship has great merit. This is because a goal of ever-higher levels of customer satisfaction is one objective on which both labor and management can agree. This shared purpose of pleasing the customer also diminishes the feeling common among workers that management is out to get all it can for itself alone.

- Single versus multiunit businesses. Service businesses are often structured with multiple identical units. Chain restaurant operations are an example. They provide good early candidates to demonstrate the potentials of a WWEW, since it would be easy to compare the results of those units converted to WWEWs with the company's other traditionally managed units. Also, it gives any such multiple-unit company the opportunity to test the WWEW in a few units before committing their entire operation to it.

- Owner adaptability. Some owners are so steeped in the traditional win-lose style of management and so locked into win-lose in their own personal outlooks and beliefs they lack the ability to change. Such was the case with Big Steel when faced with the superior performance of Nucor's employees. This points up a need for owners of a prospective WWEW to be individuals able to adapt to change. The more adaptable, the better.

- Staff adaptability. Long-unionized companies that have productivity—limiting work rules and many older employees who are set in their ways—are perhaps the least likely candidates for implementation of a WWEW, if they are candidates at all. In any company desiring to implement a WWEW, what is needed, especially at the start, are employees who can adapt to change. This is another reason service businesses tend to be among the best candidates for the implementation of a WWEW.

- Number of employees. There is likely a given number of employees—not too large, not too small—that favors ease of implementing the WWEW at the present time. While this number is yet to be determined with any degree of certitude, a reasonable guess might be somewhere between forty and one hundred employees.

- Niche cases. Notwithstanding all of the above, there are undoubtedly cases where, for example, some small manufacturers may have developed a high-enough level of mutual trust with their employees that they can go forward with the implementation of a WWEW in spite of the slow feedback loops and other deterrents that might otherwise apply.

As Experience Accumulates

There are certainly other considerations beyond those noted that may affect the challenge involved in installing a WWEW in various businesses. These will come to light as experience accumulates. As this occurs, assigning approximate index numbers for various categories of businesses will become more appropriate. For the time being, parties interested in creating a WWEW in their own businesses can likely guess fairly accurately the extent of the challenge they face by considering each of the preceding factors.

PART II
Lessons from the Great Recession

CHAPTER 9

The Wisdom of Small Teams

In their best-selling business book, *The Wisdom of Teams*, the authors, Jon Katzenbach and Douglas Smith, devote a chapter to "High-Performance Teams." They describe them as teams that emerge only occasionally and exceed all reasonable expectations. They "even surprise themselves." Such high performance is attributed by the authors to "interpersonal commitment" among such a team's members. One high-performance team member even describes this commitment as "a form of love." Another noted, "Not only did we trust each other, not only did we respect each other, but we gave a damn about the rest of the people on this team. If we saw somebody vulnerable, we were there to help."

During the recession that began in 2007–08, Santa Fe hotels were especially hard-hit because for so many hotel guests, their visits were totally discretionary. For those trying to trim expenses, eliminating a trip to the city different, as Santa Fe is known, was an easy decision. No less a problem at the Inn of the Governors was our failure to maintain our 137 percent revpar advantage over our competitors that we had achieved just before the downturn began. Even in a severely depressed economy, logic suggests we should have maintained this relative advantage. Between both declines, our team at the Inn had obviously suffered a loss of energy. Analysis of this problem revealed several probable causes.

One major factor had to be that the amount of the staffs' gainsharing distributions went down even faster than it had gone up. A more appropriate response to this issue is addressed in chapter 10, "A Time for Painsharing."

When the 2008 recession began, we had no crystal ball to tell us how deep it would become. Like others, we watched and waited to see when it would hit bottom. While this was painful, the positive side has been that it prompted us to take a hard look for ways to improve our WWEWs. One key conclusion was a point we had clearly overlooked: that eighty to one-hundred-member teams could not possibly have been as effective as many small teams engaged in friendly competition.

We had missed this for the same reason Deming missed it. He was dealing with companies that were still stuck in the cross-purposes and disaffection of win-lose management This works to limit teamwork among frontline workers to single-purpose ad hoc teams, the members of which are, hopefully, highly compatible. Even with that, however, such teams are disbanded as soon as their purposes are hopefully achieved. What we had missed was that, with all of our staff members already rowing the boat in the same direction as management, we had the infrastructure in place for ongoing ever-better teamwork We could create teams with multiple, sequential purposes, unlimited by any timeline in which new objectives could be added and positive interactions between team members could continue to grow. Compared to the traditional workplace, this is an advantage of the WWEW the full potential of which has yet to be determined.

I had noticed during our ride up to our 137 percent revpar advantage a number of inefficiencies attributable to our large eighty- to one-hundred-member teams. They included, among other things, an ongoing decline in the ideas deposited in our "bright idea" boxes at both properties, as well as a tendency of some staff members to let others do the heavy lifting in efforts to continually improve our operations.

What also surprised me was the failure of many staff members to show the strong interest I had expected in workshops provided on company time to help them improve their basic life skills. In spite of what most already saw as remarkable performance at the Inn, we were obviously not tapping several potentials. Although our people were clearly outperforming the staffs at competing hotels, we lacked the peer pressure I had expected among all of our staff members to take our performance to ever-higher levels. Instead, I could see among some of our staff a tendency to rest on our laurels, an attitude that is usually a precursor of decline.

As I looked further, I became increasingly aware that what we needed to resolve this issue and consistently improve our performance was the peer pressure that, seemingly, only friendly competition among small teams could produce. When I presented that conclusion to our staffs at both locations, I was most gratified to find they heartily agreed. We were on our way to a major upgrade of the WWEW.

It struck me as totally logical that high-performance teams would emerge only as rarities in businesses where labor and management were trying to row their boats in different directions. The psychological divide they had to cross to achieve the kind of cooperation we already enjoyed was both deep and wide. Thus was our starting point another highly significant benefit of the WWEW. And while I did not expect teamwork "exceeding all reasonable expectations" to be a short-term reality, it framed a goal all of our small teams could aspire to from the beginning.

For example, once our small teams were established, the members seemed eager to develop skills among themselves to allow them to compete with our other small teams. In short sessions before a shift began, team leaders could review key elements of people-connecting skills or problem-solving techniques that team members could use with each other on their shift, abilities they could further refine through online support. For example, the small teams learned that people-connecting skills were just as useful and powerful when used among their own team members as when used with customers, and that problem-solving skills were most effective when applied to a problem by a small, highly cohesive team. Small teams were encouraged to put suggestions for improvement in the "bright ideas" box both so they wouldn't forget them and also to enable others to share in them. In this way, upgrades of products and services could be made fully effective more quickly.

What Large Teams Cannot Accomplish

While I had long recognized that large teams could commit to a common purpose, such as providing outstanding products and services to all of our customers, large teams are not structured to commit to lesser, more specific goals. An example at the Inn is improving the quality and cost of our housekeeping. Many of the large team members at the Inn had never walked the hotel corridors or seen the interiors of our guest rooms. However, an eight-member team, all of whom were involved in housekeeping, could not only accept improving the quality and cost of housekeeping and the specific goals uncovered by our performance tracking system but could also detect and address lesser goals that might become apparent in the process.

In the same way, small teams in all of the departments at the property could commit to specific goals in their departments brought to light both by our performance tracking and their own observations to improve quality and lower costs. At the Inn, these departments include, besides housekeeping, the front desk and office, revenue management and marketing, maintenance and, in the restaurant, the kitchen or back of the house, and the servers and others in the front of the house. The performance goals of all of these departmental teams no longer remained vague but could be tied not only to the larger goal of providing "outstanding products and services to all of our customers" but to more specific goals.

Further Considerations

For a small team to pursue its shared goals and continue to accept or frame new ones, it needs to meet regularly from time to time. We quickly discovered that for most small teams, weekly meetings were too frequent, and monthly meetings were in most cases not frequent enough to maintain continuity. For most, biweekly meetings were about right. That gave them time to test and measure proposals for improvement and to identify related goals that needed tending. For certain less active teams, such as revenue management and marketing, team meetings once a month seemed sufficient.

There is an occasional need for temporary cross-functional teams to deal with specific issues that affect the entire hotel or restaurant. Once such problems are addressed and resolved, these teams disband.

Another consideration is that most employees in service businesses are not used to actively participate in teamwork in the workplace. Few have ever contributed ideas to such meetings as those described. Also, some are not totally fluent in English, which leaves them hesitant to speak up even with help from a translator.

Summary

Overall, the shift from large teams of eighty to one hundred people into small teams of five to twelve members has been well received at both the Inn of the Governors and the Waterway Cafe.

All of these small teams soon agreed on their shared purpose and, with minimum help, started developing specific goals that flowed from this shared purpose. Most of these goals will result in incremental improvements in products or services and, not to be overlooked, higher gainsharing distributions.

CHAPTER 10

A Time for Painsharing

While the reader has seen much attention paid to gainsharing, Ken Iverson of Nucor was a staunch believer, whenever appropriate, in what he termed "painsharing." During the fairly severe recession of 1982, his managers and top executives took personal income reductions of 50 percent to 60 percent—somewhat more of a reduction than the average frontline worker. Iverson himself took a reduction in his salary from $450,000 to $110,000. When told that he was listed as the lowest paid CEO of all Fortune 500 companies, his reaction was that, under the circumstances, he would have been ashamed to have received more.

As the recession that began in 2007–08 started to impact our two-service businesses in 2008, we, like most others, had little idea of how severe the downturn would become. Nor did we know how long it might be before the national economy and the revenue at our two businesses in particular would stabilize and subsequently start to improve.

We watched this revenue, especially our room revenue in Santa Fe, decline month after month versus its continual growth the year earlier, wondering when the decline would hit bottom. The dollar amount of monthly gainsharings also went into a tailspin. We took some measures to try to soften it, but by the time conditions appeared to stabilize, our $670 per month gainsharing reached at the Inn in 2008 had completely disappeared. At that point, to help maintain employee morale, we implemented a $100 minimum monthly gainsharing.

As we reached this low point in Santa Fe, we saw that our revenue per available room (revpar), which had climbed to 137 percent of the downtown average before the recession arrived, had declined to about 110 percent. This sent us the message that considerable energy had gone out of our system. This conclusion was unavoidable, given the obvious logic that we should have maintained our relative 137 percent revpar advantage over our competition.

During this decline, however, while some of the staffs hours had been slightly reduced, there had been no layoffs. Surprisingly, our staffs' already-low turnover rate had actually gone down a bit further, indicating that staff members were concerned about holding on to their jobs. This concern about job security was surely intensified by the drastic decline in the gainsharing.

Searching for a Way to Stabilize the Gainsharing

Our after-the-fact reaction to this decline was that we owners should not have allowed the gainsharing to go down as fast or as far as it did. Just as a company's stock that has appreciated over a substantial period of time tends to decline much faster than it went up if the company runs into hard times, our gainsharing at the Inn had followed the same pattern. We concluded that the 70 percent of increased profits on which the gainsharing was based on the way up should have been changed on the way down—at the expense of the owners. As things turned out, the reduction in profits absorbed by the owners on the way down should likely have been increased to probably 50 percent to balance the "pain" felt by the staff. Our one positive thought in all of this was that the Great Recession that had come upon us seemed unlikely to repeat anytime in the near future. In any case, we wanted to be ready with a plan.

One alternative approach was based on the fact that many economists cautioned that our national economy could be expected to operate at a new—and lower—norm for the next several years because of the drag created by the oversupply of housing. This "new norm" suggested in turn that we might simply lower the earlier-established owners' baseline; above the new lower baseline, the original gainsharing formula would still apply. Our concern with this approach, however, was that once we began changing this baseline, it could have negative longer-term impacts on owners as well as staff. Lowering it would not be well-received by the owners, while restoring it later, as future conditions might justify, would not likely be understood or appreciated by our staffs. So we did not opt for modifying the original owners' baseline.

Instead, at both properties we are currently adjusting our gainsharing payouts to reflect a fifty-fifty sharing of the recent pain. This should result immediately in a monthly gainsharing to employees at both locations of $150 to $250. Together with the impacts of the new small-team program just described—the positive results of which we are now beginning to see—we expect to create even more positive energy among our staffs than existed after we first adopted the original gainsharing formula in 2004–05.

From the events of the last few years, we have learned that the gainsharing formula needs to be more flexible than we anticipated. When a time for painsharing arrives, the owners need to step up to the plate. *Sharing* is the key word here. This implies, as with a marriage, that the partners need to share both the good times and the bad. The owners need to absorb at least half of the pain and, depending on the circumstances, perhaps more.

ENDPIECE

The Long-Term Potentials of the Workplace Where Everyone Wins

> *A human being experiences himself as something separated from the rest—a sort of optical delusion of his consciousness. This delusion is a kind of prison, restricting us to our personal desires and to affection for a few persons nearest to us. Our task must be to free ourselves from this prison by widening our circle of compassion to embrace all living creatures.*
> —Albert Einstein

A Basic Realignment of Capitalism

Our concern in the preceding pages has related primarily to the short-to-medium-term benefits of operating a business as a win-win model of capitalism versus the traditional win-lose model. But putting aside these short-to-medium-term benefits for a moment, simply ask, "When a far superior option is available, how much sense does it make to operate a business with a system that is not only far less productive than it might be, but one that generates distrust and disunity between its major players?" The far-superior option is the above noted win-win model. Its major economic benefits are described at the start of the preface.

Admittedly, at present, long-embedded cross-purposes and related distrust between these major players—labor and management—restricts access to this win-win option for all-too-many businesses. That obstacle, however, can and likely will be overcome as awareness of the benefits of the win-win model spreads throughout the ranks of both labor and management.

Logically, any owner starting out in business today with full awareness of the benefits of this win-win model would not opt for the traditional win-lose alternative. Yet, we are so accustomed to seeing and using and judging the relative performance of wrongheaded win-lose models that even detached observers, unaware that a win-win alternative exists, are not likely to stop and ask the all-important questions: "Isn't there a better way? Can't the problems associated with our traditional management approach be reframed as signals of opportunity to create a superior system, one able to produce far better results?"

The answer to both questions is not only yes, but that a highly successful first-generation version of this superior system was developed and put in use more than seventy-five years ago by an Ohio manufacturer, the Lincoln Electric Company. Prompted by one of their employees—amidst hard times—to question their then-existing system, Lincoln's management obviously pursued an investigation of higher potentials. The result: a remarkably successful win-win system that is, by now, little-understood history.

Unfortunately, it has taken the better part of a century to finally identify why others failed to follow Lincoln's lead. On the one hand, other manufacturers, seeing labor's usual distrust of management as too great an obstacle to surmount, might be excused for dismissing Lincoln's success as an anomaly. But that was just the start. On the other hand, Lincoln's use of piecework seemed to preempt any service applications. Now, seventy-five years after Lincoln first broke the win-lose mold, two service organizations have demonstrated that, by relating employee bonuses to teamwork rather than piecework, Lincoln's basic approach could not only work in service businesses but work wonders. The real game changer, however, is the finding that because service companies enjoy far faster feedback loops than manufacturers, they can overcome the worker distrust issue with relative ease.

This ease of overcoming worker distrust implies that if the win-win system first introduced by Lincoln is ever to spread throughout our economy, the process needs to begin in the service sector. That is where the "low-hanging fruit" exists that must be picked first to demonstrate the benefits of the system to labor and management generally. As things now stand, only repeated demonstrations of its efficacy—or competition from the likes of Lincoln and Nucor—are likely to convince those companies on the highest branches of the tree—such as long-unionized manufacturers—to make the leap, if they indeed can, into the strange new territory of win-win capitalism.

Evolutionary Patterns

If seventy-five years seems a long time for Lincoln's management model to even approach recognition as a higher form of capitalism, consider this: Einstein gave us his first or special theory of relativity more than one hundred years ago. But naysayers, even among scientists, persisted for decades. Also, it has been about seventy-five years since the discovery of quantum theory. But look how long it has taken for the benefits of digital versus analog technology, products of that discovery, to reach their present levels. Such delays seem almost the rule in major evolutionary progressions.

Fortunately, one doesn't have to be a scientist to recognize the potentials of a win-win workplace. Nor does one have to unveil higher levels of knowledge in endless incremental steps before creating such a workplace. All that's really needed at this point is the discovery by both labor and management of the benefits long awaiting them. Given today's communication resources, that could happen rather quickly.

The "Down-Arrow" of Traditional Capitalism

One way to start abetting this discovery is to clearly identify the major—and growing—negatives of American win-lose capitalism. By now, these negatives should have made obvious—at least to those who address such matters—that the long-term evolution of this win-lose model has a "down arrow." That conclusion is being made evermore obvious by our present economic situation. So let's take a closer look at these negatives.

In chapter 1, "What's Wrong with Today's Workplace," mention was made of some of the major long-term trends now afflicting the American economy. These include ballooning government debt and deficits, a consistently negative balance of trade, erosion of our manufacturing base, and the declining value of our currency. One might also add some of the political negatives: disappearing bipartisanship in Washington, more emphasis on class warfare than on the American Dream and, not least, the ever-growing entitlement culture we have created. Given the economic issues that culture has by now made hard to ignore and perhaps impossible to solve, we could be facing the kind of social unrest we have recently seen bubbling up in other countries.

These negative trends present all kinds of opportunities to assign blame. And who doesn't love to assign blame and then walk away as if the problem has been solved? But as W. Edwards Deming, the quality guru whose ideas have wider implications than generally recognized, contended, "About 96% of all problems are not people problems at all. They are systems problems." And that 96 percent figure was just the last of several numeric increases Deming made to get to that number before he died in 1993. If you look closely, you'll see that he was basically right. The politicians, the fat cats, the union bosses or anyone else one might choose to blame are not where the real blame lies. These folks are just actors in a bad play.

A Story of Accelerating Decline

The root cause of most of our present economic, social, and/or political problems can be traced back rather easily to the win-lose system of management that has long endured as the accepted standard of American capitalism. And the down arrow attending this system's evolution seems to have finally caught up with us.

From the beginning in the early 1800s of the Industrial Revolution in America, the cross-purposes between owners and managers on one side, and labor on the other, have fostered a tendency on management's part to regard labor as a commodity. Many laborers were immigrants with little education or command of the English language. They were not exactly prospects to be taken on as partners. The line of least resistance for managers was to tell workers, "Leave your brains at the door and do as you're told."

As education, technology, new alliances and awareness regarding the haves and the have-nots began to evolve, the picture began to change. Labor unions arrived. Battle lines were drawn. The owners had the wealth, but the workers had the votes. Once again, the parties involved became actors in a bad play, one in which free enterprise and the goose that lays the golden eggs had their wings increasingly clipped. This was to provide, among other things, evermore entitlements for the folks with the votes.

With severely clipped wings, it became more difficult for our "golden goose" to get off the ground. Add a regulatory environment that expands every time an unfortunate incident occurs, and the cracks in American capitalism were bound to show up as the Great Recession set in. Even the American voter is starting to realize we've gone a bit overboard with entitlements and gotten ourselves into a major fix.

By now, the issue is becoming whether we have enough time to save our vaunted golden goose before it is rushed to the "intensive care unit," perhaps never to return.

The Long-Tern Alternative

With these cheery thoughts, let's look at the implied long-term potentials of the system that first appeared at Lincoln Electric during the Great Depression. With this still-evolving system and adequate time, we might just turn things around—and even ensure the robust and permanent survival of our sick goose. We should note that it is no accident that Lincoln, like very few other companies, remains independent, alive, and well more than a 150 years after its founding in 1895.

The good news for Lincoln's philosophy is that, with blockages on its potential spread now understood, it may finally enjoy an evolutionary potential to spread across the land. Just as important are implications that the evolution of this potential would enjoy a strong up arrow.

The most telling evidence of this up arrow goes back to 1933 and the immediate, dramatic success of Lincoln's approach. That success left no doubt that its win-win model of capitalism had "legs." Almost instantly, it displaced the lack of enthusiastic cooperation typical of workers in win-lose organizations with high levels of motivation, cooperation, commitment, and even creativity. As described in the preface, all kinds of good things resulted when the company, defying convention, started awarding the lion's share of increasing short-term company profits to the people doing the work. This not only led to much happier and far more productive employees but more and more delighted customers and, in turn, increasingly happy owners. It was as if someone had sprinkled "gold dust" on the company.

The evolutionary up arrow we can observe with Lincoln's reversal of normal procedure can be projected all the way out to the imperative stated by Einstein at the start of this endpiece. His goal of human beings widening their "circles of compassion" is most interesting for several reasons. First of all, it constitutes the same path of behavioral evolution urged upon us by other serious thinkers—as well as most religions. Further, there is a clear line of logic along which the growing trust and respect generated by win-win capitalism may well evolve into the kind of compassion Einstein saw as an imperative.

Coincidentally and rather surprisingly, the same outcome turns up in the book, *The Wisdom of Teams*, as a natural and normal function of higher levels of teamwork. Achieving such teamwork consistently is the hoped-for outcome of the latest refinement of Lincoln's philosophy.

There is another aspect of Lincoln's approach that, in a historical context, is of no small significance: It is that its higher win-win model of capitalism does not impose upon anyone even a hint of the divisive limits on individual liberty, entrepreneurship, personal wealth, or ownership of property that appear in socialism and/or communism. As is the ideal of capitalism, the marketplace is where these limits are determined.

The Role of the Workplace

Along with this role of the marketplace, the workplace, obviously central to the economic potentials of this higher model of capitalism, is also key to intangible potentials as well. After all, the workplace is where most of us spend the major part of our discretionary time and, not to be overlooked, where we have the greatest opportunity to develop positive relationships with others. It is also where we have the greatest opportunity to further our personal evolution through the continual improvement of, among other things, our problem-solving and people-connecting skills.

In win-lose management, helping one's employees develop these skills would likely be considered a little strange. In win-win management, it is simply a highly logical avenue to ever-higher levels of staff performance.

To the extent this effort succeeds, it has the potential to develop, especially through teamwork, not only ever-greater economic rewards but, perhaps, more meaningful than we now understand, dramatic and ever-greater intangible potentials. Whether these higher intangible potentials will be realized among increasing numbers of people is yet to be determined. But even the suggestion of this possibility is encouraging.

Perhaps the point for now is that if humanity, either individually or collectively, is ever to evolve to a point of graduation to a transcending level of existence, the workplace is arguably the most logical arena for such a progression to take root.

JEFFERSON F. VANDER WOLK

Notable and Quotable

From George Willis, retired (1992) chairman and CEO of the Lincoln Electric Company:

"We're not a marketing company, we're not an R and D company, and we're not a service company. We're a manufacturing company, and I believe we are the best manufacturing company in the world."

EPILOGUE

The Four Pioneers of the WWEW

Much of the structure and operation of the "workplace where everyone wins" is based on the four men I consider the pioneers of this organizational model. Although I have referenced each of them and some of their ideas throughout this book, I would like to paint a more detailed picture of each of these pioneers and how they came to create their innovative management systems.

My earliest and most basic influence came from James F. Lincoln. So he is described first. W. Edwards Deming is second because he was the first to fully elaborate and draw attention to several basic management principles that underlie and support the incentive management systems of the other three pioneers. Nucor's F. Kenneth Iverson and John H. McConnell of Worthington Industries came to my attention only after I began looking for other Lincoln-type organizations. While they did not relate their systems to Lincoln's, the parallels are abundantly clear.

James F. Lincoln: the Lincoln Electric Company

James F. Lincoln (1883–1965), a native of Ohio, studied electrical engineering at Ohio State University. In 1907, Lincoln joined his brother's Lincoln Electric Co. as a salesman, becoming general manager in 1914, and president from 1928 until 1954, when he became chairman of the board.

A prolific inventor, Lincoln received twenty patents; his electrical engineering background enabled him to find the technological innovations necessary to turn arc welding into a dependable and commercially viable process. Lincoln was also a prolific author, writing letters to the editors of local newspapers and pamphlets on political and social issues. He published three books on industrial economics explaining his unique profit-sharing strategy known as the Lincoln Incentive Management System.

Lincoln's religious Congregationalist upbringing—he studied for the Christian ministry—undoubtedly contributed one of the fundamental principles underlying his incentive management system. He took it from the sermon on the mount: "Do unto others as you would have them do unto you." In his 1961 book, *A New Approach to Industrial Economics*, Lincoln called this principle "the complete answer to all problems that can arise between people." A former Ohio State football star, he viewed his company as an extension of his college team, with himself as its coach, cheerleader, and chaplain.

As part of his workplace team, Lincoln formed an advisory board comprised of both managers and elected representatives of employees within each department of the firm. Its members could bring literally any issue, large or small, to the floor for discussion. This management technique was one practical outgrowth of Lincoln's goal to treat his workers as a team, and people as assets deserving respect. It was an employee member of the advisory board who felt free to ask him, "Mr. Lincoln, if we work harder, will you pay us more money?"

This advisory board has also been cited as a factor in the company's nonunion and strike-free history. A seasoned employee describing the board said, "You tell them everything you want to tell them. It's just as if you had a union, but you tell it to the top management, the chairman and the president."

As early as 1915, the year after he became general manager, Lincoln had instituted a piecework pay system. Despite detractor's claims, Lincoln's workers were often twice as productive as their counterparts in other shops, earning more than similar workers elsewhere. After his incentive system was refined and made fully inclusive, employees who worked hard, followed orders, and identified with the company and its goals could expect substantial, sometimes enormous, bonuses. In unique cases, workers' annual pay exceeded $100,000.

The hardships of the Great Depression precipitated Lincoln Electric's famous bonus plan, when Lincoln employees responded to Depression-era cuts in hours and pay by offering—through their advisory board—to work harder in exchange for a share of the company's profits.

The first year's payout, which came from profits after shareholder dividends had been paid, averaged 30 percent of each worker's regular annual pay. This incentive system continued to generate increasing productivity. Lincoln shared with his workers up to 70 percent of beyond-normal company profits. Although a discretionary policy, the annual bonus (with some modification) has remained in place since its inception.

By the mid-1930s, James Lincoln had turned his company into what a 1993 Compensation and Benefits Review article called "one of the first companies in the United States to install a successful productivity-based incentive system for all employees."

By the early 1940s, Lincoln Electric had grown to become the world's largest manufacturer of arc welding equipment, with subsidiaries in Canada, the United Kingdom, and Australia, and licensees in Mexico, Brazil, and Argentina. By 1944, Lincoln Electric's benefits package included a company-funded pension plan.

Lincoln experimented with a "guaranteed employment" policy in the post-World War II era. This arrangement was designed to preserve a skilled workforce and encourage employee suggestions for increased efficiency. According to the policy, anyone who worked at the company for two years would not be laid off.

Even after Lincoln's tenure as CEO, the incentive programs he instituted were preserved. And even during the economic crisis of the early 1980s, no one was laid off, and the company, which remained profitable, even managed to pay a bonus during those crisis years. Lincoln Electric emerged from the early 1980s downturn debt-free and profitable. It also retained its world leadership of the welding industry.

W. Edwards Deming

W. Edwards Deming (1900–93), statistician, professor, author, lecturer, and consultant, grew up on his father's farm in Wyoming. His undergraduate degree was in electrical engineering, but both his graduate degrees were in mathematics. He incorporated training by some of the best statisticians of his day in his work at the US Department of Agriculture and the Census Department.

While serving under General Douglas MacArthur as a census consultant to the Japanese government after World War II, he taught statistical process control methods to Japanese business leaders. He showed their top management how to improve their companies' design, service, product quality, testing and sales to global markets. A number of Japanese automobile and electronics manufacturers applied his techniques widely and experienced very high levels of quality and productivity. Their improved quality combined with lowered cost created new international demand for Japanese products. Deming witnessed that country's rapid economic growth—an increase he had predicted would come quickly as a result of applying statistical techniques. He is regarded as having had more impact upon Japanese manufacturing and business than any other individual of non-Japanese heritage. Despite being considered something of a hero in Japan, he was only just beginning to win recognition in the United States at the time of his death. Dr. Deming's teachings and philosophy can best be seen through the results they produced in Japan. There, the Deming Prize, Japanese industry's most coveted award, continues to exert considerable influence on the disciplines of quality control and quality management.

Deming authored *Out of the Crisis* (1982) and *The New Economics for Industry, Government, Education* (1993), which includes his system of profound knowledge and his fourteen points for management.

Deming was rabid in a constructive sense about cooperation between labor and management. He claimed a company could succeed only if labor and management shared a common purpose. For him, there could only be one shared purpose for any company, and that purpose had to be total customer satisfaction. While many American companies proclaim their commitment to such customer satisfaction, only a few have managed to adopt Deming's complete system based on the continual improvement of products and services. The seeming reasons: lack of leadership continuity and insufficient worker incentives.

Ironically, the key elements of Deming's philosophy—the shared purpose of labor and management (customer satisfaction) and the continual improvement of products and services—evolved naturally at Lincoln, Worthington, and Nucor as functions of their high profit-sharing incentives. Deming's philosophy has been made a formal component of the "workplace where everyone wins" because it codifies his major elements from the start. Applying these key elements will keep managers ahead of the curve when putting a WWEW in place.

F. Kenneth Iverson: the Nucor Corporation

Ken Iverson (1925–2002), with degrees in aeronautical and mechanical engineering, started with the Nuclear Corporation of America as a part-time consultant with the goal of identifying the most promising division of the organization. When he chose the one making steel joists, named Vulcraft (later changed to Nucor), the owners offered him the job of running it. Iverson accepted and joined the company as vice president in 1962. At the time, this "promising" division was part of a larger sick company with a history of mediocrity. Impressed by Iverson's success, the board would later ask him to become the company's president. Iverson accepted the challenge.

His basic strategy was to focus the company's activities on its one profitable division, steel joists, and to become the low-cost manufacturer serving the company's joist market. He invested capital in modern technology and ongoing research. But his true genius was in his psychology as seen in his human relations plan. It was designed to lower costs by increasing labor productivity.

Iverson developed a plan that would give the worker an opportunity for increased pay and stable employment. He felt this could be accomplished by raising the level of labor productivity to the point where Nucor could make higher quality products, underprice the competition, and at the same time pay higher wages and salaries than other steel companies.

His compensation system was based on performance bonuses, offered in a manner that promoted teamwork and loyalty. Everyone at the plant was included in the bonus payment system, even Iverson.

Most potentially divisive signs of status were eliminated. For example, all executives ate in the company cafeteria with everyone else; any fringe benefits given to managers were also given to hourly workers; executives flew in coach, not first class. And any hourly worker who had a problem with a manager could take the complaint directly to Iverson.

Within two years, Iverson made the Nuclear Corporation profitable. By the end of 1968, the company opened two additional truss plants: one in Norfolk, Nebraska (1966) and another in Jewett, Texas (1968).

For the next sixteen years, the company that became Nucor in 1972 had sales and earnings that grew so rapidly the company became a symbol of what was still right about American industry.

Nucor did have a few down years, such as 1975 and 1982. But even then, the company earned a profit and avoided layoffs, while the major steel companies were showing huge losses and laying off workers.

For Nucor's production workers, the basic incentive was a weekly bonus tied to measurable output in the 1970s. The plan grouped production workers into teams of twenty-five to thirty employees. Each team was given a production goal based on 90 percent of the output historically produced during a full week of work. At the end of the week, actual output was compared with the 90 percent quota. To the extent that actual output exceeded the quota, a bonus was paid. The bonus was proportional to the amount by which output actually exceeded the goal. That made it possible for a group to earn a bonus equal to 100 percent or more of the base wage. In 1980, for example, the standard for melting and casting was ten tons an hour (the same as ten years earlier). Workers were paid a 4 percent bonus for every ton over that. During a six-month stretch of time that year, Nucor workers averaged thirty tons an hour. As a result, they were paid wages equal to 180 percent of their base wage. And those bonuses were paid on a weekly basis, thus providing immediate reinforcement for the superior performance.

In 1985, a *Reader's Digest* article reported that, "Nucor's hourly employees average over $40,000 annually, about $5,000 more than their unionized counterparts at big steel mills—when they can get work. In the rural areas where Nucor builds its plants, the average factory worker makes less than half that amount."[1]

The deep double-dip recession of 1980–82 provided a rare opportunity to observe Iverson's job security mechanism under conditions of extreme stress. A huge drop in demand for domestic steel caused the major companies to eliminate thousands of jobs. The crisis made its deepest impact on Nucor in 1982 when the company had to cut production in half. This was done by reducing the workweek to four days. As a result, the average Nucor worker's earnings fell by 25 percent while department heads took a 40 percent cut, and general managers and officers had their earnings reduced by 55 to 60 percent. In stark contrast to the competition, Nucor maintained employment and asked all employees to share the pain by accepting temporary pay cuts.

John H. McConnell: Worthington Industries

Near the top of a one-page statement of corporate philosophy for Worthington Industries, founder John H. McConnell (1923–2008) wrote, "Our Golden Rule: We treat our customers, employees, investors and suppliers as we would like to be treated." When asked about this, he once commented, "Everyone knows that the Golden Rule works for spouses, families and friends. Why wouldn't it hold true for our jobs?"

---

[1] Fortney, David L., "The Little Steel Mill that Could," *Readers Digest*, August 1985, pp. 110–11.

McConnell grew up within a working-class family in West Virginia as a hardworking, loyal employee in a manufacturing plant, where he learned how management should not treat employees. When he founded the Worthington Steel Company, he brought with him a respect for his workers and an appreciation for the heart they put into their work. "I feel deeply that people should be treated well not because they are tools for building a successful company," he said, "but because they are valuable as human beings."

"Without my employees," he said, "Worthington Industries is nothing."

"There is no science to management," he said. "When leaders are involved with their people instead of only being involved in paperwork, they not only feel more effective, they are more effective."

"The most vital trait any leader can have is the ability to recognize that every person in every department wants most of all to be seen as a human being with needs and desires that are not much different than his or her own."

In his eyes, his profit-sharing plan is all about recognizing the contribution and true value of those who do the work.

Fortune Magazine considered Worthington to be among the top one hundred best companies to work for in 2004. They wrote, "No time clocks in these steel-processing plants. Workers get profit-sharing payouts ranging from 40% to 70% of base pay, and the company pays 100% of health insurance premiums for employees and family members."

From its first year, the Worthington Steel Company had an incentive program of some sort. In the beginning, incentives were based on "tons of steel shipped," which was very effective in encouraging productivity. In 1960, the incentive basis shifted to a more equitable formula. Today, payouts are based on bottom-line profits. Incentive is tied to salary so that each employee is motivated to improve his or her position in the company. Payouts also are given in cash rather than in benefits or stock, since any deferred incentives would not generate the day-to-day productivity everyone desired. "Unless employees see a direct correlation between their contribution and their reward," McConnell said, "an incentive program doesn't make sense."

At Worthington, there is full financial transparency. Executives share financial information with employees in simple and clear ways. With a profit-sharing plan in place, it is important for employees to understand where their efforts are headed and be able to react quickly to areas of the company where they can help improve profitability.

In small seminars, employees get short courses in minifinance and economics. They get to give up popular misconceptions about how much of a company's gross income is actually profit. People are shown how employee-controlled cost factors like scrap rate, absenteeism, rejection rates, and equipment and supply usage have an effect on the bottom line.

The year Worthington introduced profit-sharing, all employees were put on salary, in effect elevating all plant people to the same level as those working in the office. As a result, profit-sharing began to create healthy peer pressure. People police themselves; they are conscientious about costs and waste, and there are few abuses of the salary plan.

There are no official coffee breaks at Worthington, but plenty of free coffee whenever someone needs it. In other words, the production line never comes to a complete stop in order for everyone to stop working and enjoy a recess at the same time. Employees are treated as adults with job responsibility. As a result, Worthington enjoys better productivity, lower turnover, and a long line of applicants for every open position.

The Worthington employees never formed a union or voted to form one. "I have a disdain for labor unions," McConnell once said. "And I'm embarrassed that companies treated their employees so poorly that unions were forced to form."

"From the beginning, when I founded Worthington Steel," McConnell said, "I wanted to reward employees for their hard work. I always saw employees as my partners. If they succeeded, I succeeded. If they came up with better ideas, we all benefited. I made sure of that."

ACKNOWLEDGEMENTS

In creating the two "workplaces where everyone wins" addressed herein, I must express my thanks for the untiring cooperation of both the staffs and the managers of these businesses, especially Rich Gagliardi, general manager of the Waterway Cafe, who was on hand at its 1986 opening; Charlotte Sliva, general manager of the Inn of the Governors for fifteen years; and her successor, Sam Gerberding. The ideas and feedback provided by these managers and their staffs have been invaluable to this effort.

Other major contributors: Dr. Louis Savary, who is responsible for over one hundred books and whose unending help and punctuality were key in producing this book. Dr. Fred Nanni, chairman of the division of accounting and law at Babson College, who has provided ongoing constructive suggestions throughout this effort. Clare Crawford-Mason and Lloyd Dobyns, quality pioneers whose familiarity with W. Edwards Deming provided the focus needed to apply many of Deming's ideas. William Glavin, former president of Babson College who initially brought me into the Deming circle. Matthew Cross, our gifted leader in pursuing life-skills training for all of our staff members. My son, Peter Vander Wolk, and his talented associate, Scott Fogarty, who will soon be out promoting the WWEW.

Others who lent help and/or encouragement: Curt Blake, founder of Friendly Ice Cream; Bob Maginn, CEO of Jenzibar Inc.; my long-standing friend, Dr. Michael Gzasko of Sante Fe; Debbi Wraga, our exceptional publisher contact; and Kate Fogarty, for her help in editing.

Last but certainly not least are the thanks due my devoted wife, Betty, for her fifty-three years of support and, most recently, both the aid she has lent to this effort and her gracious hosting in our homes of several of those involved.

APPENDIX A

The performance-tracking format used as a driver of the WWEW showing the operating profit at the Inn of the Governors from 2004 to 2008 and of Del Charro, the Inn's food-and-beverage operation, for the same period.

INN OF THE GOVERNORS NET OPERATING PROFIT
(000'S OMITTED) MONTHLY HISTORIES

	2003	2004	2005	2006	2007	2008
January	(27)	20	8	37	21	51
February	18	60	43	76	115	56
March	106	110	131	125	174	196
April	67	152	202	162	211	213
May	194	205	196	242	273	308
June	165	222	250	268	308	335
July	265	315	358	325	396	412
August	379	348	385	435	468	494
September	219	243	282	274	311	310
October	272	295	306	330	356	307
November	60	94	84	105	118	108
December	85	89	142	120	152	135

JEFFERSON F. VANDER WOLK

TRAILING TWELVE-MONTH TREND

	2003	2004	2005	2006	2007	2008
January		1850	2141	2416	2483	2935
February		1892	2124	2449	2522	2876
March		1896	2145	2443	2571	2898
April		1981	2195	2403	2621	2899
May		1992	2186	2449	2652	2934
June		2049	2214	2467	2692	2961
July		2099	2257	2434	2763	2977
August		2068	2294	2484	2796	3002
September		2092	2333	2476	2834	3001
October		2115	2344	2500	2860	2952
November	1718	2149	2334	2521	2873	2941
December	1803	2153	2387	2499	2905	2924

INN OF THE GOVERNORS'S FOOD-AND-BEVERAGE
DEPARTMENTAL PROFIT MONTHLY HISTORIES

	2003	2004	2005	2006	2007	2008
January	13.0	29.0	27.0	47.0	36.1	39.9
February	21.0	32.0	30.0	53.0	40.6	35.3
March	19.0	29.0	35.0	49.0	54.8	55.5
April	17.0	32.0	47.0	50.0	51.3	62.1
May	27.0	48.0	54.0	57.0	60.6	77.3
June	13.0	49.0	59.0	59.0	62.2	73.7
July	39.0	56.0	62.0	56.0	63.3	83.2
August	44.0	43.0	57.0	58.0	64.2	86.9
September	37.0	36.0	64.0	45.0	51.2	58.0
October	39.0	42.0	49.0	45.0	50.0	46.1
November	20.0	27.0	49.0	41.4	38.8	55.9
December	24.0	37.0	58.0	46.5	56.0	65.4

THE WORKPLACE WHERE EVERYONE WINS

TRAILING TWELVE-MONTH TREND

	2003	2004	2005	2006	2007	2008
January		329.0	458.0	611.0	596.0	632.9
February		340.0	456.0	634.0	583.7	627.6
March		350.0	462.0	648.0	589.5	628.3
April		365.0	477.0	651.0	590.8	639.1
May		386.0	483.0	654.0	594.4	655.8
June		422.0	493.0	654.0	597.6	667.4
July		439.0	499.0	648.0	604.9	687.2
August		438.0	513.0	649.0	611.1	709.9
September		437.0	541.0	630.0	617.3	716.7
October		440.0	548.0	626.0	622.3	712.8
November		447.0	570.0	618.4	619.6	729.9
December	313.0	460.0	591.0	606.9	629.2	739.3

BIBLIOGRAPHY

Dawson, Virginia. *Lincoln Electric: A History*. Cleveland: The Lincoln Electric Company, 1999.

Deming, W. Edwards. *Out of the Crisis: Principles for the Transformation of Western Management*. Cambridge, MA: MIT Center for Advanced Engineering Study, 1982.

Dobyns, Lloyd, and Clare Crawford-Mason. *Quality OR ELSE: The Revolution in World Business*. Boston: Houghton Mifflin, 1991.

———. *Thinking About Quality: Progress, Wisdom and the Deming Philosophy*. New York: Times Books, 1994.

Iverson, Ken. *Plain Talk: Lessons from a Business Maverick (Chairman of Nucor Corporation)*. New York: John Wiley, 1998.

Katzenbach, Jon R., and Zia Khan. *Leading Outside the Lines: How to Mobilize the Informal Organization, Energize Your Team, and Get Better Results*. San Francisco: Jossey-Bass, 2010.

Katzenbach, Jon R., and Douglas K. Smith. *The Wisdom of Teams: Creating the High-Performance Organization*. Boston: Harvard Business School Press, 1993. Also published by Harper Business, 1994.

Richard I, Jr., Kirkland. "Pilgrim's Progress at Nucor," *Fortune*, April 6, 1981, p. 44.

Koller, Frank. *SPARK: Lessons from Lincoln Electric's Unique Guaranteed Employment Program (How Old-Fashioned Values Drive a Twenty-First-Century Corporation)*. New York: Public Affairs Press, 2010.

Maciariello, Joseph A. *Lasting Value: Lessons from a Century of Agility at Lincoln Electric*. New York: John Wiley, 2000.

McConnell, John. *Our Golden Rule (The Philosophy of Worthington Industries)*. Columbus, OH: Franklin University Press, 2004.

McManus, George J. "Everybody Shares the Pie at Nucor," *Iron Age*, October 1986.

Scherkenbach, William W. *The Deming Route to Quality and Productivity: Road Maps and Roadblocks*. Washington DC: CEE Press (George Washington University), 1986.

Walton, Mary. *The Deming Management Method (Foreword by W. Edwards Deming)*. New York: Dodd, Mead, 1986.

THE REASON FOR THIS BOOK

Using two service businesses—a 100-room hotel in downtown Santa Fe and a 350-seat restaurant in Palm Beach Gardens, Florida—as experimental laboratories, the author tells how, with the enthusiastic support of their staffs, these two businesses were turned into uniquely profitable "workplaces where everyone wins." This was achieved with a landmark management system never before thought applicable to service organizations. These businesses demonstrated, however, that not only can this landmark system work wonders in service but that the service sector is where it needs to be applied first if its huge but little-understood potential is ever to be realized.

ABOUT THE AUTHOR

Jefferson F. Vander Wolk, a native of Massachusetts, attended Phillips Exeter Academy, Yale University, and Babson College. During a Korean War tour of duty as an air force instructor pilot in West Texas, he formed a construction company to build homes and, later, rental apartment and commercial projects. At age thirty-five, he semiretired on the East Coast to pursue interests in related management and problem-solving methodologies.

During his college years, he had become familiar with the Lincoln Electric Company and its highly successful management system. A later visit with that company's president, James F. Lincoln, led to an enduring interest in Lincoln's approach. This long-standing interest, combined with what he viewed as a mistaken belief that Lincoln's approach would never work in service businesses, finally prompted him in 2004 to establish two "management laboratories" to qualify that contention. What these two laboratories demonstrated is the inspiration for this book.

www.ingramcontent.com/pod-product-compliance
Lightning Source LLC
Chambersburg PA
CBHW030847180526
45163CB00004B/1478